D1796967

Social Technologies
Complete Self-Assessment Guide

The guidance in this Self-Assessment is based on Social Technologies best practices and standards in business process architecture, design and quality management. The guidance is also based on the professional judgment of the individual collaborators listed in the Acknowledgments.

Notice of rights

Trademarks

Copyright © by The Art of Service
http://theartofservice.com
service@theartofservice.com

Table of Contents

About The Art of Service

The Art of Service, Business Process Architects since 2000, is dedicated to helping stakeholders achieve excellence.

Defining, designing, creating, and implementing a process to solve a stakeholders challenge or meet an objective is the most valuable role… In EVERY group, company, organization and department.

Unless you're talking a one-time, single-use project, there should be a process. Whether that process is managed and implemented by humans, AI, or a combination of the two, it needs to be designed by someone with a complex enough perspective to ask the right questions.

Someone capable of asking the right questions and step back and say, 'What are we really trying to accomplish here? And is there a different way to look at it?'

With The Art of Service's Standard Requirements Self-Assessments, we empower people who can do just that — whether their title is marketer, entrepreneur, manager, salesperson, consultant, Business Process Manager, executive assistant, IT Manager, CIO etc... —they are the people who rule the future. They are people who watch the process as it happens, and ask the right questions to make the process work better.

Contact us when you need any support with this Self-Assessment and any help with templates, blue-prints and examples of standard documents you might need:

http://theartofservice.com
service@theartofservice.com

Included Resources - how to access

Included with your purchase of the book is the Social

Technologies Self-Assessment Spreadsheet Dashboard which contains all questions and Self-Assessment areas and auto-generates insights, graphs, and project RACI planning - all with examples to get you started right away.

How? Simply send an email to
access@theartofservice.com
with this books' title in the subject to get the Social Technologies Self Assessment Tool right away.

You will receive the following contents with New and Updated specific criteria:

- The latest quick edition of the book in PDF

- The latest complete edition of the book in PDF, which criteria correspond to the criteria in...

- The Self-Assessment Excel Dashboard, and...

- Example pre-filled Self-Assessment Excel Dashboard to get familiar with results generation

- In-depth specific Checklists covering the topic

- Project management checklists and templates to assist with implementation

Purpose of this Self-Assessment

This Self-Assessment has been developed to improve understanding of the requirements and elements of Social Technologies, based on best practices and standards in business process architecture, design and quality management.

It is designed to allow for a rapid Self-Assessment to determine how closely existing management practices and procedures correspond to the elements of the Self-Assessment.

The criteria of requirements and elements of Social Technologies have been rephrased in the format of a Self-Assessment questionnaire, with a seven-criterion scoring system, as explained in this document.

In this format, even with limited background knowledge of Social Technologies, a manager can quickly review existing operations to determine how they measure up to the standards. This in turn can serve as the starting point of a 'gap analysis' to identify management tools or system elements that might usefully be implemented in the organization to help improve overall performance.

How to use the Self-Assessment

On the following pages are a series of questions to identify to what extent your Social Technologies initiative is complete in comparison to the requirements set in standards.

To facilitate answering the questions, there is a space in front of each question to enter a score on a scale of '1' to '5'.

1 Strongly Disagree

2 Disagree

3 Neutral

4 Agree

5 Strongly Agree

Read the question and rate it with the following in front of mind:

'In my belief, the answer to this question is clearly defined'.

There are two ways in which you can choose to interpret this statement;
1.   how aware are you that the answer to the question is clearly defined
2.   for more in-depth analysis you can choose to gather evidence and confirm the answer to the question. This obviously will take more time, most Self-Assessment users opt for the first way to interpret the question and dig deeper later on based on the outcome of the overall Self-Assessment.

A score of '1' would mean that the answer is not clear at all, where a '5' would mean the answer is crystal clear and defined. Leave emtpy when the question is not applicable or you don't want to answer it, you can skip it without affecting your score. Write your score in the space provided.

After you have responded to all the appropriate statements in each section, compute your average score for that section, using the formula provided, and round to the nearest tenth. Then transfer to the corresponding spoke in the Social Technologies Scorecard on the second next page of the Self-Assessment.

Your completed Social Technologies Scorecard will give you a clear presentation of which Social Technologies areas need attention.

Social Technologies Scorecard Example

Example of how the finalized Scorecard can look like:

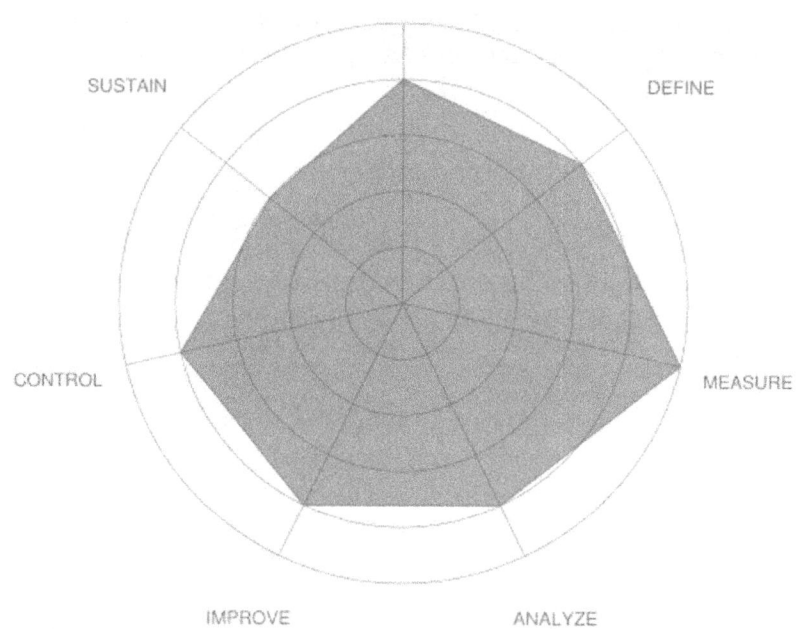

Social Technologies Scorecard

Your Scores:

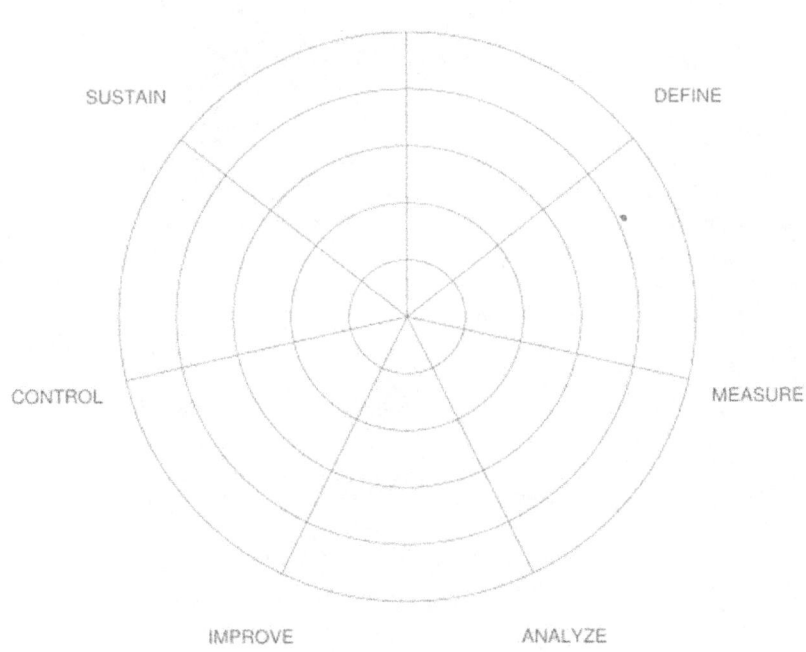

BEGINNING OF THE SELF-ASSESSMENT:

CRITERION #1: RECOGNIZE

INTENT: Be aware of the need for change. Recognize that there is an unfavorable variation, problem or symptom.

In my belief, the answer to this question is clearly defined:

5 Strongly Agree

4 Agree

3 Neutral

2 Disagree

1 Strongly Disagree

1. How do you recognize an social technologies objection?
<--- Score

2. Looking at each person individually – does every one have the qualities which are needed to work in this group?
<--- Score

3. Are problem definition and motivation clearly presented?
<--- Score

4. Who needs budgets?
<--- Score

5. What should be considered when identifying available resources, constraints, and deadlines?
<--- Score

6. Why is this needed?
<--- Score

7. Does the problem have ethical dimensions?
<--- Score

8. What social technologies problem should be solved?
<--- Score

9. Whom do you really need or want to serve?
<--- Score

10. What are the social technologies resources needed?
<--- Score

11. What needs to be done?
<--- Score

12. What situation(s) led to this social technologies Self Assessment?
<--- Score

13. What vendors make products that address the

social technologies needs?
<--- Score

14. What social technologies capabilities do you need?
<--- Score

15. Are employees recognized for desired behaviors?
<--- Score

16. To what extent does each concerned units management team recognize social technologies as an effective investment?
<--- Score

17. Will a response program recognize when a crisis occurs and provide some level of response?
<--- Score

18. Is the quality assurance team identified?
<--- Score

19. What is the smallest subset of the problem you can usefully solve?
<--- Score

20. Is it needed?
<--- Score

21. How much are sponsors, customers, partners, stakeholders involved in social technologies? In other words, what are the risks, if social technologies does not deliver successfully?
<--- Score

22. What activities does the governance board need

to consider?
<--- Score

23. What tools and technologies are needed for a custom social technologies project?
<--- Score

24. Can management personnel recognize the monetary benefit of social technologies?
<--- Score

25. Is the need for organizational change recognized?
<--- Score

26. Is it clear when you think of the day ahead of you what activities and tasks you need to complete?
<--- Score

27. For your social technologies project, identify and describe the business environment, is there more than one layer to the business environment?
<--- Score

28. Are there recognized social technologies problems?
<--- Score

29. Does your organization need more social technologies education?
<--- Score

30. Who defines the rules in relation to any given issue?
<--- Score

31. Which issues are too important to ignore?

<--- Score

32. How do you recognize an objection?
<--- Score

33. How do you assess your social technologies workforce capability and capacity needs, including skills, competencies, and staffing levels?
<--- Score

34. Do you recognize social technologies achievements?
<--- Score

35. What problems are you facing and how do you consider social technologies will circumvent those obstacles?
<--- Score

36. Have you identified your social technologies key performance indicators?
<--- Score

37. When a social technologies manager recognizes a problem, what options are available?
<--- Score

38. What are the timeframes required to resolve each of the issues/problems?
<--- Score

39. What is the recognized need?
<--- Score

40. Do you need different information or graphics?
<--- Score

41. Are controls defined to recognize and contain problems?

<--- Score

42. Will new equipment/products be required to facilitate social technologies delivery, for example is new software needed?

<--- Score

43. What else needs to be measured?

<--- Score

44. Will it solve real problems?

<--- Score

45. What is the problem or issue?

<--- Score

46. Who are your key stakeholders who need to sign off?

<--- Score

47. What are the stakeholder objectives to be achieved with social technologies?

<--- Score

48. What is the extent or complexity of the social technologies problem?

<--- Score

49. What creative shifts do you need to take?

<--- Score

50. Where do you need to exercise leadership?

<--- Score

51. How do you take a forward-looking perspective in identifying social technologies research related to market response and models?
<--- Score

52. As a sponsor, customer or management, how important is it to meet goals, objectives?
<--- Score

53. Think about the people you identified for your social technologies project and the project responsibilities you would assign to them, what kind of training do you think they would need to perform these responsibilities effectively?
<--- Score

54. Are employees recognized or rewarded for performance that demonstrates the highest levels of integrity?
<--- Score

55. What would happen if social technologies weren't done?
<--- Score

56. Consider your own social technologies project, what types of organizational problems do you think might be causing or affecting your problem, based on the work done so far?
<--- Score

57. What is the social technologies problem definition? What do you need to resolve?
<--- Score

58. Does social technologies create potential expectations in other areas that need to be recognized and considered?
<--- Score

59. What are your needs in relation to social technologies skills, labor, equipment, and markets?
<--- Score

60. Do you know what you need to know about social technologies?
<--- Score

61. Who needs to know?
<--- Score

62. Who needs to know about social technologies?
<--- Score

63. Who else hopes to benefit from it?
<--- Score

64. Who needs what information?
<--- Score

65. How can auditing be a preventative security measure?
<--- Score

66. How are you going to measure success?
<--- Score

67. What prevents you from making the changes you know will make you a more effective social technologies leader?
<--- Score

68. Which information does the social technologies business case need to include?
<--- Score

69. How do you identify the kinds of information that you will need?
<--- Score

70. Do you have/need 24-hour access to key personnel?
<--- Score

71. Would you recognize a threat from the inside?
<--- Score

72. What are the expected benefits of social technologies to the stakeholder?
<--- Score

73. What are the minority interests and what amount of minority interests can be recognized?
<--- Score

74. Did you miss any major social technologies issues?
<--- Score

75. Which needs are not included or involved?
<--- Score

76. What extra resources will you need?
<--- Score

77. Why the need?
<--- Score

78. Are there regulatory / compliance issues?
<--- Score

79. Do you need to avoid or amend any social technologies activities?
<--- Score

80. Are your goals realistic? Do you need to redefine your problem? Perhaps the problem has changed or maybe you have reached your goal and need to set a new one?
<--- Score

81. To what extent would your organization benefit from being recognized as a award recipient?
<--- Score

82. Are there social technologies problems defined?
<--- Score

83. What does social technologies success mean to the stakeholders?
<--- Score

84. What resources or support might you need?
<--- Score

85. Are there any specific expectations or concerns about the social technologies team, social technologies itself?
<--- Score

86. Are you dealing with any of the same issues today

as yesterday? What can you do about this?
<--- Score

87. Will social technologies deliverables need to be tested and, if so, by whom?
<--- Score

88. What are the clients issues and concerns?
<--- Score

89. How are the social technologies's objectives aligned to the group's overall stakeholder strategy?
<--- Score

90. How do you identify subcontractor relationships?
<--- Score

91. What needs to stay?
<--- Score

92. How are training requirements identified?
<--- Score

93. What do employees need in the short term?
<--- Score

94. What is the problem and/or vulnerability?
<--- Score

95. What information do users need?
<--- Score

96. What social technologies coordination do you need?
<--- Score

97. How many trainings, in total, are needed?
<--- Score

98. What do you need to start doing?
<--- Score

Add up total points for this section:
_____ = Total points for this section

Divided by: _____ (number of
statements answered) = _____
Average score for this section

Transfer your score to the social
technologies Index at the beginning of
the Self-Assessment.

CRITERION #2: DEFINE:

INTENT: Formulate the stakeholder problem. Define the problem, needs and objectives.

In my belief, the answer to this question is clearly defined:

5 Strongly Agree

4 Agree

3 Neutral

2 Disagree

1 Strongly Disagree

1. Is social technologies linked to key stakeholder goals and objectives?
<--- Score

2. When are meeting minutes sent out? Who is on the distribution list?
<--- Score

3. What is the context?

<--- Score

4. Has the social technologies work been fairly and/or equitably divided and delegated among team members who are qualified and capable to perform the work? Has everyone contributed?
<--- Score

5. If substitutes have been appointed, have they been briefed on the social technologies goals and received regular communications as to the progress to date?
<--- Score

6. Is the current 'as is' process being followed? If not, what are the discrepancies?
<--- Score

7. What are the dynamics of the communication plan?
<--- Score

8. Are required metrics defined, what are they?
<--- Score

9. Is there a social technologies management charter, including stakeholder case, problem and goal statements, scope, milestones, roles and responsibilities, communication plan?
<--- Score

10. Is the improvement team aware of the different versions of a process: what they think it is vs. what it actually is vs. what it should be vs. what it could be?
<--- Score

11. How do you gather social technologies requirements?

<--- Score

12. How do you manage unclear social technologies requirements?
<--- Score

13. Who defines (or who defined) the rules and roles?
<--- Score

14. What are the Roles and Responsibilities for each team member and its leadership? Where is this documented?
<--- Score

15. What are the record-keeping requirements of social technologies activities?
<--- Score

16. What social technologies requirements should be gathered?
<--- Score

17. What is out of scope?
<--- Score

18. How have you defined all social technologies requirements first?
<--- Score

19. Who is gathering social technologies information?
<--- Score

20. Is the team equipped with available and reliable resources?
<--- Score

21. Are all requirements met?
<--- Score

22. What are the requirements for audit information?
<--- Score

23. Is there regularly 100% attendance at the team meetings? If not, have appointed substitutes attended to preserve cross-functionality and full representation?
<--- Score

24. What customer feedback methods were used to solicit their input?
<--- Score

25. How did the social technologies manager receive input to the development of a social technologies improvement plan and the estimated completion dates/times of each activity?
<--- Score

26. Are there different segments of customers?
<--- Score

27. Where can you gather more information?
<--- Score

28. What are the boundaries of the scope? What is in bounds and what is not? What is the start point? What is the stop point?
<--- Score

29. How will the social technologies team and

the group measure complete success of social technologies?
<--- Score

30. Has a team charter been developed and communicated?
<--- Score

31. How and when will the baselines be defined?
<--- Score

32. How is the team tracking and documenting its work?
<--- Score

33. How do you catch social technologies definition inconsistencies?
<--- Score

34. Do the problem and goal statements meet the SMART criteria (specific, measurable, attainable, relevant, and time-bound)?
<--- Score

35. What is in scope?
<--- Score

36. How do you manage scope?
<--- Score

37. The political context: who holds power?
<--- Score

38. How will variation in the actual durations of each activity be dealt with to ensure that the expected social technologies results are met?

<--- Score

39. What is the definition of success?
<--- Score

40. Why are you doing social technologies and what is the scope?
<--- Score

41. Are audit criteria, scope, frequency and methods defined?
<--- Score

42. What baselines are required to be defined and managed?
<--- Score

43. Is there any additional social technologies definition of success?
<--- Score

44. In what way can you redefine the criteria of choice clients have in your category in your favor?
<--- Score

45. Are the social technologies requirements complete?
<--- Score

46. Are approval levels defined for contracts and supplements to contracts?
<--- Score

47. Has a social technologies requirement not been met?
<--- Score

48. What is the scope of social technologies?
<--- Score

49. What sort of initial information to gather?
<--- Score

50. How do you gather the stories?
<--- Score

51. Are the social technologies requirements testable?
<--- Score

52. Are different versions of process maps needed to account for the different types of inputs?
<--- Score

53. Are roles and responsibilities formally defined?
<--- Score

54. What are the social technologies use cases?
<--- Score

55. Who is gathering information?
<--- Score

56. What is out-of-scope initially?
<--- Score

57. Is there a critical path to deliver social technologies results?
<--- Score

58. How does the social technologies manager ensure against scope creep?
<--- Score

59. Is the social technologies scope manageable?
<--- Score

60. What would be the goal or target for a social technologies's improvement team?
<--- Score

61. Is scope creep really all bad news?
<--- Score

62. How was the 'as is' process map developed, reviewed, verified and validated?
<--- Score

63. Have all basic functions of social technologies been defined?
<--- Score

64. What happens if social technologies's scope changes?
<--- Score

65. How would you define the culture at your organization, how susceptible is it to social technologies changes?
<--- Score

66. What are the social technologies tasks and definitions?
<--- Score

67. What scope to assess?
<--- Score

68. Have all of the relationships been defined

properly?
<--- Score

69. What information should you gather?
<--- Score

70. What constraints exist that might impact the team?
<--- Score

71. How are consistent social technologies definitions important?
<--- Score

72. Are resources adequate for the scope?
<--- Score

73. Does the team have regular meetings?
<--- Score

74. What are the rough order estimates on cost savings/opportunities that social technologies brings?
<--- Score

75. What scope do you want your strategy to cover?
<--- Score

76. What are (control) requirements for social technologies Information?
<--- Score

77. Who are the social technologies improvement team members, including Management Leads and Coaches?
<--- Score

78. Is the work to date meeting requirements?
<--- Score

79. Who approved the social technologies scope?
<--- Score

80. Is the team adequately staffed with the desired cross-functionality? If not, what additional resources are available to the team?
<--- Score

81. What knowledge or experience is required?
<--- Score

82. What is a worst-case scenario for losses?
<--- Score

83. Does the scope remain the same?
<--- Score

84. Will a social technologies production readiness review be required?
<--- Score

85. What specifically is the problem? Where does it occur? When does it occur? What is its extent?
<--- Score

86. Is it clearly defined in and to your organization what you do?
<--- Score

87. What are the tasks and definitions?
<--- Score

88. How can the value of social technologies be

defined?
<--- Score

89. Do you all define social technologies in the same way?
<--- Score

90. What sources do you use to gather information for a social technologies study?
<--- Score

91. Has the improvement team collected the 'voice of the customer' (obtained feedback – qualitative and quantitative)?
<--- Score

92. Is there a completed, verified, and validated high-level 'as is' (not 'should be' or 'could be') stakeholder process map?
<--- Score

93. Is there a clear social technologies case definition?
<--- Score

94. Are task requirements clearly defined?
<--- Score

95. Is the social technologies scope complete and appropriately sized?
<--- Score

96. How often are the team meetings?
<--- Score

97. When is the estimated completion date?

<--- Score

98. Has anyone else (internal or external to the group) attempted to solve this problem or a similar one before? If so, what knowledge can be leveraged from these previous efforts?
<--- Score

99. When is/was the social technologies start date?
<--- Score

100. How would you define social technologies leadership?
<--- Score

101. What was the context?
<--- Score

102. Is there a completed SIPOC representation, describing the Suppliers, Inputs, Process, Outputs, and Customers?
<--- Score

103. How do you build the right business case?
<--- Score

104. What key stakeholder process output measure(s) does social technologies leverage and how?
<--- Score

105. Have the customer needs been translated into specific, measurable requirements? How?
<--- Score

106. What critical content must be communicated – who, what, when, where, and how?

<--- Score

107. What are the compelling stakeholder reasons for embarking on social technologies?
<--- Score

108. Is social technologies required?
<--- Score

109. Is special social technologies user knowledge required?
<--- Score

110. Has/have the customer(s) been identified?
<--- Score

111. How do you gather requirements?
<--- Score

112. What information do you gather?
<--- Score

113. Are customer(s) identified and segmented according to their different needs and requirements?
<--- Score

114. Has a project plan, Gantt chart, or similar been developed/completed?
<--- Score

115. What is the definition of social technologies excellence?
<--- Score

116. Do you have organizational privacy requirements?

<--- Score

117. What system do you use for gathering social technologies information?
<--- Score

118. Scope of sensitive information?
<--- Score

119. Are there any constraints known that bear on the ability to perform social technologies work? How is the team addressing them?
<--- Score

120. How do you think the partners involved in social technologies would have defined success?
<--- Score

121. Has a high-level 'as is' process map been completed, verified and validated?
<--- Score

122. What is the worst case scenario?
<--- Score

123. Has everyone on the team, including the team leaders, been properly trained?
<--- Score

124. Has the direction changed at all during the course of social technologies? If so, when did it change and why?
<--- Score

125. Are accountability and ownership for social technologies clearly defined?

<--- Score

126. How do you keep key subject matter experts in the loop?
<--- Score

127. Is the scope of social technologies defined?
<--- Score

128. What is in the scope and what is not in scope?
<--- Score

129. What social technologies services do you require?
<--- Score

130. Is social technologies currently on schedule according to the plan?
<--- Score

131. What is the scope of the social technologies effort?
<--- Score

132. What gets examined?
<--- Score

133. What defines best in class?
<--- Score

134. What intelligence can you gather?
<--- Score

135. Do you have a social technologies success story or case study ready to tell and share?
<--- Score

136. Has your scope been defined?
<--- Score

137. Is data collected and displayed to better understand customer(s) critical needs and requirements.
<--- Score

Add up total points for this section:
_ _ _ _ _ = Total points for this section

Divided by: _ _ _ _ _ _ (number of statements answered) = _ _ _ _ _ _ Average score for this section

Transfer your score to the social technologies Index at the beginning of the Self-Assessment.

CRITERION #3: MEASURE:

In my belief, the answer to this
question is clearly defined:

5 Strongly Agree

4 Agree

3 Neutral

2 Disagree

1 Strongly Disagree

1. Have design-to-cost goals been established?
<--- Score

2. How do you verify performance?
<--- Score

3. What could cause you to change course?
<--- Score

4. How much does it cost?
<--- Score

5. How do you verify social technologies completeness and accuracy?
<--- Score

6. How do you verify if social technologies is built right?
<--- Score

7. What is the total cost related to deploying social technologies, including any consulting or professional services?
<--- Score

8. What are the costs?
<--- Score

9. How will your organization measure success?
<--- Score

10. What disadvantage does this cause for the user?
<--- Score

11. How are measurements made?
<--- Score

12. Where is the cost?
<--- Score

13. What happens if cost savings do not materialize?
<--- Score

14. Are you aware of what could cause a problem?

<--- Score

15. Does a social technologies quantification method exist?
<--- Score

16. How do you aggregate measures across priorities?
<--- Score

17. Has a cost center been established?
<--- Score

18. What details are required of the social technologies cost structure?
<--- Score

19. What are the current costs of the social technologies process?
<--- Score

20. How long to keep data and how to manage retention costs?
<--- Score

21. What harm might be caused?
<--- Score

22. How do you verify and develop ideas and innovations?
<--- Score

23. What can be used to verify compliance?
<--- Score

24. What drives O&M cost?
<--- Score

25. At what cost?
<--- Score

26. How can you reduce costs?
<--- Score

27. When should you bother with diagrams?
<--- Score

28. Are you able to realize any cost savings?
<--- Score

29. What is your social technologies quality cost segregation study?
<--- Score

30. Who is involved in verifying compliance?
<--- Score

31. Are the units of measure consistent?
<--- Score

32. Are social technologies vulnerabilities categorized and prioritized?
<--- Score

33. Have you included everything in your social technologies cost models?
<--- Score

34. Are there measurements based on task performance?
<--- Score

35. Is the cost worth the social technologies effort

?

<--- Score

36. What are your key social technologies organizational performance measures, including key short and longer-term financial measures?

<--- Score

37. How do you measure lifecycle phases?

<--- Score

38. What do people want to verify?

<--- Score

39. Are the measurements objective?

<--- Score

40. What are your customers expectations and measures?

<--- Score

41. What is the cost of rework?

<--- Score

42. What does a Test Case verify?

<--- Score

43. How sensitive must the social technologies strategy be to cost?

<--- Score

44. How do you verify your resources?

<--- Score

45. What is the root cause(s) of the problem?

<--- Score

46. What are the estimated costs of proposed changes?
<--- Score

47. How will success or failure be measured?
<--- Score

48. What are the uncertainties surrounding estimates of impact?
<--- Score

49. Do the benefits outweigh the costs?
<--- Score

50. How can you manage cost down?
<--- Score

51. What would it cost to replace your technology?
<--- Score

52. What are your operating costs?
<--- Score

53. How will effects be measured?
<--- Score

54. Is the solution cost-effective?
<--- Score

55. Are you taking your company in the direction of better and revenue or cheaper and cost?
<--- Score

56. How do your measurements capture actionable social technologies information for use in exceeding

your customers expectations and securing your customers engagement?
<--- Score

57. How do you measure variability?
<--- Score

58. Where can you go to verify the info?
<--- Score

59. Which costs should be taken into account?
<--- Score

60. How can you reduce the costs of obtaining inputs?
<--- Score

61. What methods are feasible and acceptable to estimate the impact of reforms?
<--- Score

62. How do you measure efficient delivery of social technologies services?
<--- Score

63. Among the social technologies product and service cost to be estimated, which is considered hardest to estimate?
<--- Score

64. What measurements are possible, practicable and meaningful?
<--- Score

65. Which social technologies impacts are significant?
<--- Score

66. What are the costs and benefits?
<--- Score

67. What are the social technologies investment costs?
<--- Score

68. What are hidden social technologies quality costs?
<--- Score

69. Do you aggressively reward and promote the people who have the biggest impact on creating excellent social technologies services/products?
<--- Score

70. What does verifying compliance entail?
<--- Score

71. What is the total fixed cost?
<--- Score

72. What is measured? Why?
<--- Score

73. Which measures and indicators matter?
<--- Score

74. How do you verify the authenticity of the data and information used?
<--- Score

75. What causes investor action?
<--- Score

76. How do you quantify and qualify impacts?
<--- Score

77. How is progress measured?

<--- Score

78. How can you measure the performance?

<--- Score

79. How to cause the change?

<--- Score

80. How do you verify and validate the social technologies data?

<--- Score

81. What does losing customers cost your organization?

<--- Score

82. Is it possible to estimate the impact of unanticipated complexity such as wrong or failed assumptions, feedback, etcetera on proposed reforms?

<--- Score

83. Are indirect costs charged to the social technologies program?

<--- Score

84. What are your primary costs, revenues, assets?

<--- Score

85. What are the social technologies key cost drivers?

<--- Score

86. How are costs allocated?

<--- Score

87. How do you measure success?
<--- Score

88. When are costs are incurred?
<--- Score

89. What are the costs of delaying social technologies action?
<--- Score

90. What does your operating model cost?
<--- Score

91. What causes mismanagement?
<--- Score

92. Will social technologies have an impact on current business continuity, disaster recovery processes and/or infrastructure?
<--- Score

93. What relevant entities could be measured?
<--- Score

94. Who should receive measurement reports?
<--- Score

95. Does the social technologies task fit the client's priorities?
<--- Score

96. How will you measure your social technologies effectiveness?
<--- Score

97. Do you have an issue in getting priority?

<--- Score

98. Was a business case (cost/benefit) developed?
<--- Score

99. What would be a real cause for concern?
<--- Score

100. What is your decision requirements diagram?
<--- Score

101. Are there any easy-to-implement alternatives to social technologies? Sometimes other solutions are available that do not require the cost implications of a full-blown project?
<--- Score

102. What are the operational costs after social technologies deployment?
<--- Score

103. What measurements are being captured?
<--- Score

104. What could cause delays in the schedule?
<--- Score

105. What are the types and number of measures to use?
<--- Score

106. Does management have the right priorities among projects?
<--- Score

107. How is performance measured?

<--- Score

108. What are you verifying?
<--- Score

109. Where is it measured?
<--- Score

110. What potential environmental factors impact the social technologies effort?
<--- Score

111. How frequently do you track social technologies measures?
<--- Score

112. What are the costs of reform?
<--- Score

113. Are there competing social technologies priorities?
<--- Score

114. Did you tackle the cause or the symptom?
<--- Score

115. What do you measure and why?
<--- Score

116. How do you prevent mis-estimating cost?
<--- Score

117. Who pays the cost?
<--- Score

118. What is an unallowable cost?

<--- Score

119. What causes innovation to fail or succeed in your organization?
<--- Score

120. Do you verify that corrective actions were taken?
<--- Score

121. Do you have any cost social technologies limitation requirements?
<--- Score

122. Do you have a flow diagram of what happens?
<--- Score

123. Why do the measurements/indicators matter?
<--- Score

124. How can a social technologies test verify your ideas or assumptions?
<--- Score

125. Are actual costs in line with budgeted costs?
<--- Score

126. How will measures be used to manage and adapt?
<--- Score

127. What is the cause of any social technologies gaps?
<--- Score

128. Are missed social technologies opportunities costing your organization money?

<--- Score

129. How will costs be allocated?
<--- Score

130. What are the strategic priorities for this year?
<--- Score

131. How do you control the overall costs of your work processes?
<--- Score

132. Are the social technologies benefits worth its costs?
<--- Score

133. What are allowable costs?
<--- Score

134. Do you effectively measure and reward individual and team performance?
<--- Score

135. How can you measure social technologies in a systematic way?
<--- Score

136. How do you verify the social technologies requirements quality?
<--- Score

137. How will you measure success?
<--- Score

Add up total points for this section:
_ _ _ _ _ = Total points for this section

Divided by: _____ (number of
statements answered) = _____
Average score for this section

Transfer your score to the social
technologies Index at the beginning of
the Self-Assessment.

CRITERION #4: ANALYZE:

INTENT: Analyze causes, assumptions and hypotheses.

In my belief, the answer to this question is clearly defined:

5 Strongly Agree

4 Agree

3 Neutral

2 Disagree

1 Strongly Disagree

1. Did any additional data need to be collected?
<--- Score

2. How do your work systems and key work processes relate to and capitalize on your core competencies?
<--- Score

3. Have you defined which data is gathered how?
<--- Score

4. Identify an operational issue in your organization, for example, could a particular task be done more quickly or more efficiently by social technologies?
<--- Score

5. What is the oversight process?
<--- Score

6. What kind of crime could a potential new hire have committed that would not only not disqualify him/her from being hired by your organization, but would actually indicate that he/she might be a particularly good fit?
<--- Score

7. How much data can be collected in the given timeframe?
<--- Score

8. What are the social technologies design outputs?
<--- Score

9. Where is the data coming from to measure compliance?
<--- Score

10. What qualifications are necessary?
<--- Score

11. How do you identify specific social technologies investment opportunities and emerging trends?
<--- Score

12. A compounding model resolution with available relevant data can often provide insight towards a

solution methodology; which social technologies models, tools and techniques are necessary?
<--- Score

13. What are your best practices for minimizing social technologies project risk, while demonstrating incremental value and quick wins throughout the social technologies project lifecycle?
<--- Score

14. Is data and process analysis, root cause analysis and quantifying the gap/opportunity in place?
<--- Score

15. How does the organization define, manage, and improve its social technologies processes?
<--- Score

16. Do staff qualifications match your project?
<--- Score

17. What do you need to qualify?
<--- Score

18. What qualifications do social technologies leaders need?
<--- Score

19. Who owns what data?
<--- Score

20. What process improvements will be needed?
<--- Score

21. What does the data say about the performance of the stakeholder process?

<--- Score

22. How do you use social technologies data and information to support organizational decision making and innovation?
<--- Score

23. Should you invest in industry-recognized qualifications?
<--- Score

24. How do you ensure that the social technologies opportunity is realistic?
<--- Score

25. What are the processes for audit reporting and management?
<--- Score

26. How do mission and objectives affect the social technologies processes of your organization?
<--- Score

27. What tools were used to narrow the list of possible causes?
<--- Score

28. Were there any improvement opportunities identified from the process analysis?
<--- Score

29. How often will data be collected for measures?
<--- Score

30. Have any additional benefits been identified that will result from closing all or most of the gaps?

<--- Score

31. Did any value-added analysis or 'lean thinking' take place to identify some of the gaps shown on the 'as is' process map?
<--- Score

32. Has data output been validated?
<--- Score

33. Do your employees have the opportunity to do what they do best everyday?
<--- Score

34. What are your current levels and trends in key social technologies measures or indicators of product and process performance that are important to and directly serve your customers?
<--- Score

35. How do you define collaboration and team output?
<--- Score

36. What output to create?
<--- Score

37. Are gaps between current performance and the goal performance identified?
<--- Score

38. What successful thing are you doing today that may be blinding you to new growth opportunities?
<--- Score

39. What controls do you have in place to protect

data?
<--- Score

40. How will corresponding data be collected?
<--- Score

41. Was a cause-and-effect diagram used to explore the different types of causes (or sources of variation)?
<--- Score

42. How is the social technologies Value Stream Mapping managed?
<--- Score

43. Was a detailed process map created to amplify critical steps of the 'as is' stakeholder process?
<--- Score

44. What are the best opportunities for value improvement?
<--- Score

45. What other jobs or tasks affect the performance of the steps in the social technologies process?
<--- Score

46. What is your organizations system for selecting qualified vendors?
<--- Score

47. What information qualified as important?
<--- Score

48. What is the Value Stream Mapping?
<--- Score

49. What methods do you use to gather social technologies data?
<--- Score

50. What conclusions were drawn from the team's data collection and analysis? How did the team reach these conclusions?
<--- Score

51. How will the social technologies data be captured?
<--- Score

52. What are your outputs?
<--- Score

53. What did the team gain from developing a sub-process map?
<--- Score

54. How is social technologies data gathered?
<--- Score

55. Are social technologies changes recognized early enough to be approved through the regular process?
<--- Score

56. Is there any way to speed up the process?
<--- Score

57. What are the disruptive social technologies technologies that enable your organization to radically change your business processes?
<--- Score

58. What quality tools were used to get through the analyze phase?

<--- Score

59. How do you implement and manage your work processes to ensure that they meet design requirements?
<--- Score

60. What are evaluation criteria for the output?
<--- Score

61. Who is involved in the management review process?
<--- Score

62. Is there an established change management process?
<--- Score

63. What is the output?
<--- Score

64. What types of data do your social technologies indicators require?
<--- Score

65. Do your contracts/agreements contain data security obligations?
<--- Score

66. What data do you need to collect?
<--- Score

67. Where can you get qualified talent today?
<--- Score

68. What social technologies data do you gather or

use now?

<--- Score

69. What are the revised rough estimates of the financial savings/opportunity for social technologies improvements?

<--- Score

70. What are the personnel training and qualifications required?

<--- Score

71. What are the social technologies business drivers?

<--- Score

72. Can you add value to the current social technologies decision-making process (largely qualitative) by incorporating uncertainty modeling (more quantitative)?

<--- Score

73. Which social technologies data should be retained?

<--- Score

74. Where is social technologies data gathered?

<--- Score

75. How will the data be checked for quality?

<--- Score

76. What process should you select for improvement?

<--- Score

77. Is the suppliers process defined and controlled?

<--- Score

78. What social technologies data should be managed?
<--- Score

79. How can risk management be tied procedurally to process elements?
<--- Score

80. What training and qualifications will you need?
<--- Score

81. How was the detailed process map generated, verified, and validated?
<--- Score

82. What resources go in to get the desired output?
<--- Score

83. What qualifications and skills do you need?
<--- Score

84. Is the performance gap determined?
<--- Score

85. What qualifications are needed?
<--- Score

86. How difficult is it to qualify what social technologies ROI is?
<--- Score

87. When should a process be art not science?
<--- Score

88. What tools were used to generate the list of

possible causes?
<--- Score

89. Is the final output clearly identified?
<--- Score

90. Is pre-qualification of suppliers carried out?
<--- Score

91. Think about the functions involved in your social technologies project, what processes flow from these functions?
<--- Score

92. Have the problem and goal statements been updated to reflect the additional knowledge gained from the analyze phase?
<--- Score

93. What social technologies data should be collected?
<--- Score

94. Who is involved with workflow mapping?
<--- Score

95. Do you have the authority to produce the output?
<--- Score

96. Who gets your output?
<--- Score

97. Were any designed experiments used to generate additional insight into the data analysis?
<--- Score

98. What are the necessary qualifications?
<--- Score

99. Record-keeping requirements flow from the records needed as inputs, outputs, controls and for transformation of a social technologies process, are the records needed as inputs to the social technologies process available?
<--- Score

100. What data is gathered?
<--- Score

101. How is the data gathered?
<--- Score

102. Were Pareto charts (or similar) used to portray the 'heavy hitters' (or key sources of variation)?
<--- Score

103. What is the complexity of the output produced?
<--- Score

104. How do you promote understanding that opportunity for improvement is not criticism of the status quo, or the people who created the status quo?
<--- Score

105. Do several people in different organizational units assist with the social technologies process?
<--- Score

106. What are your key performance measures or indicators and in-process measures for the control and improvement of your social technologies

processes?
<--- Score

107. What will drive social technologies change?
<--- Score

108. What were the crucial 'moments of truth' on the process map?
<--- Score

109. What were the financial benefits resulting from any 'ground fruit or low-hanging fruit' (quick fixes)?
<--- Score

110. Who will gather what data?
<--- Score

111. Do your leaders quickly bounce back from setbacks?
<--- Score

112. How are outputs preserved and protected?
<--- Score

113. What is the cost of poor quality as supported by the team's analysis?
<--- Score

114. Do quality systems drive continuous improvement?
<--- Score

115. Do you, as a leader, bounce back quickly from setbacks?
<--- Score

116. What is your organizations process which leads to recognition of value generation?

<--- Score

117. Are you missing social technologies opportunities?

<--- Score

118. What is the social technologies Driver?

<--- Score

119. Are all staff in core social technologies subjects Highly Qualified?

<--- Score

120. Is there a strict change management process?

<--- Score

121. What social technologies metrics are outputs of the process?

<--- Score

122. Is the gap/opportunity displayed and communicated in financial terms?

<--- Score

123. Is the social technologies process severely broken such that a re-design is necessary?

<--- Score

124. What internal processes need improvement?

<--- Score

125. An organizationally feasible system request is one that considers the mission, goals and objectives of the organization, key questions are: is the social

technologies solution request practical and will it solve a problem or take advantage of an opportunity to achieve company goals?
<--- Score

Add up total points for this section:
_ _ _ _ _ = Total points for this section

Divided by: _ _ _ _ _ _ (number of statements answered) = _ _ _ _ _ _
Average score for this section

Transfer your score to the social technologies Index at the beginning of the Self-Assessment.

CRITERION #5: IMPROVE:

INTENT: Develop a practical solution. Innovate, establish and test the solution and to measure the results.

In my belief, the answer to this question is clearly defined:

5 Strongly Agree

4 Agree

3 Neutral

2 Disagree

1 Strongly Disagree

1. Does a good decision guarantee a good outcome?
<--- Score

2. Do you cover the five essential competencies: Communication, Collaboration,Innovation, Adaptability, and Leadership that improve an organizations ability to leverage the new social technologies in a volatile global economy?
<--- Score

3. How do you improve your likelihood of success ?
<--- Score

4. What are the affordable social technologies risks?
<--- Score

5. Would you develop a social technologies Communication Strategy?
<--- Score

6. Is there any other social technologies solution?
<--- Score

7. Where do you need social technologies improvement?
<--- Score

8. Do you combine technical expertise with business knowledge and social technologies Key topics include lifecycles, development approaches, requirements and how to make a business case?
<--- Score

9. Do vendor agreements bring new compliance risk ?
<--- Score

10. Explorations of the frontiers of social technologies will help you build influence, improve social technologies, optimize decision making, and sustain change, what is your approach?
<--- Score

11. To what extent does management recognize social technologies as a tool to increase the results?
<--- Score

12. How risky is your organization?
<--- Score

13. What practices helps your organization to develop its capacity to recognize patterns?
<--- Score

14. What improvements have been achieved?
<--- Score

15. What tools were used to evaluate the potential solutions?
<--- Score

16. Is the measure of success for social technologies understandable to a variety of people?
<--- Score

17. Is there a high likelihood that any recommendations will achieve their intended results?
<--- Score

18. Who will be responsible for documenting the social technologies requirements in detail?
<--- Score

19. Who manages supplier risk management in your organization?
<--- Score

20. Who manages social technologies risk?
<--- Score

21. Why improve in the first place?
<--- Score

22. Can you integrate quality management and risk management?
<--- Score

23. Risk factors: what are the characteristics of social technologies that make it risky?
<--- Score

24. How do you improve productivity?
<--- Score

25. Was a pilot designed for the proposed solution(s)?
<--- Score

26. Who are the people involved in developing and implementing social technologies?
<--- Score

27. How do the social technologies results compare with the performance of your competitors and other organizations with similar offerings?
<--- Score

28. Was a social technologies charter developed?
<--- Score

29. How scalable is your social technologies solution?
<--- Score

30. What area needs the greatest improvement?
<--- Score

31. How do you improve social technologies service

perception, and satisfaction?
<--- Score

32. How significant is the improvement in the eyes of the end user?
<--- Score

33. What is social technologies's impact on utilizing the best solution(s)?
<--- Score

34. How will you know that a change is an improvement?
<--- Score

35. Do those selected for the social technologies team have a good general understanding of what social technologies is all about?
<--- Score

36. What lessons, if any, from a pilot were incorporated into the design of the full-scale solution?
<--- Score

37. Are risk triggers captured?
<--- Score

38. Will the controls trigger any other risks?
<--- Score

39. How do you keep improving social technologies?
<--- Score

40. What is social technologies risk?
<--- Score

41. What communications are necessary to support the implementation of the solution?
<--- Score

42. How are social technologies risks managed?
<--- Score

43. Who are the key stakeholders for the social technologies evaluation?
<--- Score

44. Where do the social technologies decisions reside?
<--- Score

45. How can you improve social technologies?
<--- Score

46. How can you better manage risk?
<--- Score

47. How do you decide how much to remunerate an employee?
<--- Score

48. Do you have the optimal project management team structure?
<--- Score

49. What to do with the results or outcomes of measurements?
<--- Score

50. Who makes the social technologies decisions in your organization?
<--- Score

51. How does the team improve its work?
<--- Score

52. How can skill-level changes improve social technologies?
<--- Score

53. Are events managed to resolution?
<--- Score

54. Who are the social technologies decision makers?
<--- Score

55. What error proofing will be done to address some of the discrepancies observed in the 'as is' process?
<--- Score

56. How do you manage and improve your social technologies work systems to deliver customer value and achieve organizational success and sustainability?
<--- Score

57. Do you need to do a usability evaluation?
<--- Score

58. What social technologies improvements can be made?
<--- Score

59. Who should make the social technologies decisions?
<--- Score

60. In the past few months, what is the smallest change you have made that has had the biggest

positive result? What was it about that small change that produced the large return?
<--- Score

61. What assumptions are made about the solution and approach?
<--- Score

62. How do you link measurement and risk?
<--- Score

63. How can the phases of social technologies development be identified?
<--- Score

64. Is the social technologies documentation thorough?
<--- Score

65. How do you measure risk?
<--- Score

66. How do you measure progress and evaluate training effectiveness?
<--- Score

67. Have you identified breakpoints and/or risk tolerances that will trigger broad consideration of a potential need for intervention or modification of strategy?
<--- Score

68. What should a proof of concept or pilot accomplish?
<--- Score

69. What attendant changes will need to be made to ensure that the solution is successful?
<--- Score

70. Are decisions made in a timely manner?
<--- Score

71. What were the underlying assumptions on the cost-benefit analysis?
<--- Score

72. What are your current levels and trends in key measures or indicators of workforce and leader development?
<--- Score

73. Are you assessing social technologies and risk?
<--- Score

74. What is the implementation plan?
<--- Score

75. How do you manage social technologies risk?
<--- Score

76. Are the key business and technology risks being managed?
<--- Score

77. Who will be responsible for making the decisions to include or exclude requested changes once social technologies is underway?
<--- Score

78. How do you deal with social technologies risk?
<--- Score

79. What went well, what should change, what can improve?

<--- Score

80. What needs improvement? Why?

<--- Score

81. What do you want to improve?

<--- Score

82. For estimation problems, how do you develop an estimation statement?

<--- Score

83. Which of the recognised risks out of all risks can be most likely transferred?

<--- Score

84. What are the concrete social technologies results?

<--- Score

85. Does the goal represent a desired result that can be measured?

<--- Score

86. What tools were used to tap into the creativity and encourage 'outside the box' thinking?

<--- Score

87. Is supporting social technologies documentation required?

<--- Score

88. What can you do to improve?

<--- Score

89. What risks do you need to manage?
<--- Score

90. How will you know when its improved?
<--- Score

91. Who controls the risk?
<--- Score

92. How do you define the solutions' scope?
<--- Score

93. What resources are required for the improvement efforts?
<--- Score

94. For decision problems, how do you develop a decision statement?
<--- Score

95. What are the expected social technologies results?
<--- Score

96. How do you mitigate social technologies risk?
<--- Score

97. What criteria will you use to assess your social technologies risks?
<--- Score

98. Is the social technologies solution sustainable?
<--- Score

99. How does your organization evaluate strategic social technologies success?
<--- Score

100. If you could go back in time five years, what decision would you make differently? What is your best guess as to what decision you're making today you might regret five years from now?
<--- Score

101. What tools do you use once you have decided on a social technologies strategy and more importantly how do you choose?
<--- Score

102. What is the magnitude of the improvements?
<--- Score

103. What strategies for social technologies improvement are successful?
<--- Score

104. Who will be using the results of the measurement activities?
<--- Score

105. What tools were most useful during the improve phase?
<--- Score

106. What are the implications of the one critical social technologies decision 10 minutes, 10 months, and 10 years from now?
<--- Score

107. Is risk periodically assessed?

<--- Score

108. How will you recognize and celebrate results?
<--- Score

109. What is the risk?
<--- Score

110. Can the solution be designed and implemented within an acceptable time period?
<--- Score

111. How will you know that you have improved?
<--- Score

112. What current systems have to be understood and/or changed?
<--- Score

113. How will you measure the results?
<--- Score

114. Who are the social technologies decision-makers?
<--- Score

115. Who do you report social technologies results to?
<--- Score

116. Have you achieved social technologies improvements?
<--- Score

117. social technologies risk decisions: whose call Is It?
<--- Score

118. When you map the key players in your own work and the types/domains of relationships with them, which relationships do you find easy and which challenging, and why?
<--- Score

119. Who controls key decisions that will be made?
<--- Score

120. How is continuous improvement applied to risk management?
<--- Score

121. Risk Identification: What are the possible risk events your organization faces in relation to social technologies?
<--- Score

122. Who do you report social technologies results to?
<--- Score

123. Is the scope clearly documented?
<--- Score

124. What is the team's contingency plan for potential problems occurring in implementation?
<--- Score

125. Is social technologies documentation maintained?
<--- Score

126. What does the 'should be' process map/design look like?
<--- Score

127. Risk events: what are the things that could go wrong?
<--- Score

128. Can you identify any significant risks or exposures to social technologies third- parties (vendors, service providers, alliance partners etc) that concern you?
<--- Score

129. What actually has to improve and by how much?
<--- Score

130. Were any criteria developed to assist the team in testing and evaluating potential solutions?
<--- Score

131. What is the social technologies's sustainability risk?
<--- Score

132. How are policy decisions made and where?
<--- Score

133. At what point will vulnerability assessments be performed once social technologies is put into production (e.g., ongoing Risk Management after implementation)?
<--- Score

134. Is the social technologies risk managed?
<--- Score

135. How can you improve performance?
<--- Score

136. How do you measure improved social technologies service perception, and satisfaction?
<--- Score

137. Are the risks fully understood, reasonable and manageable?
<--- Score

138. How do you go about comparing social technologies approaches/solutions?
<--- Score

139. What are the social technologies security risks?
<--- Score

Add up total points for this section:
_ _ _ _ _ = Total points for this section

Divided by: _ _ _ _ _ _ (number of statements answered) = _ _ _ _ _ _
Average score for this section

Transfer your score to the social technologies Index at the beginning of the Self-Assessment.

CRITERION #6: CONTROL:

INTENT: Implement the practical solution. Maintain the performance and correct possible complications.

In my belief, the answer to this question is clearly defined:

5 Strongly Agree

4 Agree

3 Neutral

2 Disagree

1 Strongly Disagree

1. Does social technologies appropriately measure and monitor risk?
<--- Score

2. Is the social technologies test/monitoring cost justified?
<--- Score

3. How do you select, collect, align, and integrate

social technologies data and information for tracking daily operations and overall organizational performance, including progress relative to strategic objectives and action plans?

<--- Score

4. How can you best use all of your knowledge repositories to enhance learning and sharing?

<--- Score

5. Are the planned controls working?

<--- Score

6. What should you measure to verify efficiency gains?

<--- Score

7. Does the response plan contain a definite closed loop continual improvement scheme (e.g., plan-do-check-act)?

<--- Score

8. Where do ideas that reach policy makers and planners as proposals for social technologies strengthening and reform actually originate?

<--- Score

9. Is there documentation that will support the successful operation of the improvement?

<--- Score

10. Who has control over resources?

<--- Score

11. Implementation Planning: is a pilot needed to test the changes before a full roll out occurs?

<--- Score

12. Will existing staff require re-training, for example, to learn new business processes?
<--- Score

13. How will input, process, and output variables be checked to detect for sub-optimal conditions?
<--- Score

14. What is your plan to assess your security risks?
<--- Score

15. Does the social technologies performance meet the customer's requirements?
<--- Score

16. Is new knowledge gained imbedded in the response plan?
<--- Score

17. What key inputs and outputs are being measured on an ongoing basis?
<--- Score

18. Have new or revised work instructions resulted?
<--- Score

19. Do you monitor the social technologies decisions made and fine tune them as they evolve?
<--- Score

20. What do you measure to verify effectiveness gains?
<--- Score

21. What are your results for key measures or indicators of the accomplishment of your social technologies strategy and action plans, including building and strengthening core competencies?
<--- Score

22. Who is the social technologies process owner?
<--- Score

23. What social technologies standards are applicable?
<--- Score

24. Can you adapt and adjust to changing social technologies situations?
<--- Score

25. Are suggested corrective/restorative actions indicated on the response plan for known causes to problems that might surface?
<--- Score

26. What adjustments to the strategies are needed?
<--- Score

27. How might the group capture best practices and lessons learned so as to leverage improvements?
<--- Score

28. How do you spread information?
<--- Score

29. How do you monitor usage and cost?
<--- Score

30. How will report readings be checked to effectively monitor performance?

<--- Score

31. You may have created your quality measures at a time when you lacked resources, technology wasn't up to the required standard, or low service levels were the industry norm. Have those circumstances changed?
<--- Score

32. Who sets the social technologies standards?
<--- Score

33. Is a response plan in place for when the input, process, or output measures indicate an 'out-of-control' condition?
<--- Score

34. Is knowledge gained on process shared and institutionalized?
<--- Score

35. How will you measure your QA plan's effectiveness?
<--- Score

36. What do your reports reflect?
<--- Score

37. Will your goals reflect your program budget?
<--- Score

38. What is the best design framework for social technologies organization now that, in a post industrial-age if the top-down, command and control model is no longer relevant?
<--- Score

39. Is reporting being used or needed?
<--- Score

40. What are the known security controls?
<--- Score

41. Are operating procedures consistent?
<--- Score

42. Who is going to spread your message?
<--- Score

43. How do you establish and deploy modified action plans if circumstances require a shift in plans and rapid execution of new plans?
<--- Score

44. Has the improved process and its steps been standardized?
<--- Score

45. Is there a transfer of ownership and knowledge to process owner and process team tasked with the responsibilities.
<--- Score

46. Is there an action plan in case of emergencies?
<--- Score

47. What is the control/monitoring plan?
<--- Score

48. How will the process owner and team be able to hold the gains?
<--- Score

49. How will new or emerging customer needs/ requirements be checked/communicated to orient the process toward meeting the new specifications and continually reducing variation?
<--- Score

50. How do controls support value?
<--- Score

51. Does job training on the documented procedures need to be part of the process team's education and training?
<--- Score

52. What should the next improvement project be that is related to social technologies?
<--- Score

53. How do you plan on providing proper recognition and disclosure of supporting companies?
<--- Score

54. Are pertinent alerts monitored, analyzed and distributed to appropriate personnel?
<--- Score

55. What are the key elements of your social technologies performance improvement system, including your evaluation, organizational learning, and innovation processes?
<--- Score

56. Does a troubleshooting guide exist or is it needed?
<--- Score

57. Is a response plan established and deployed?
<--- Score

58. Are controls in place and consistently applied?
<--- Score

59. What is your theory of human motivation, and how does your compensation plan fit with that view?
<--- Score

60. Is there a documented and implemented monitoring plan?
<--- Score

61. In the case of a social technologies project, the criteria for the audit derive from implementation objectives, an audit of a social technologies project involves assessing whether the recommendations outlined for implementation have been met, can you track that any social technologies project is implemented as planned, and is it working?
<--- Score

62. What are customers monitoring?
<--- Score

63. Is there a social technologies Communication plan covering who needs to get what information when?
<--- Score

64. Do the social technologies decisions you make today help people and the planet tomorrow?
<--- Score

65. Can support from partners be adjusted?

<--- Score

66. How will social technologies decisions be made and monitored?
<--- Score

67. How is social technologies project cost planned, managed, monitored?
<--- Score

68. Is there a control plan in place for sustaining improvements (short and long-term)?
<--- Score

69. Act/Adjust: What Do you Need to Do Differently?
<--- Score

70. What quality tools were useful in the control phase?
<--- Score

71. What other systems, operations, processes, and infrastructures (hiring practices, staffing, training, incentives/rewards, metrics/dashboards/scorecards, etc.) need updates, additions, changes, or deletions in order to facilitate knowledge transfer and improvements?
<--- Score

72. Against what alternative is success being measured?
<--- Score

73. What are the critical parameters to watch?
<--- Score

74. How do your controls stack up?
<--- Score

75. Are the planned controls in place?
<--- Score

76. Will any special training be provided for results interpretation?
<--- Score

77. Are new process steps, standards, and documentation ingrained into normal operations?
<--- Score

78. Is there a recommended audit plan for routine surveillance inspections of social technologies's gains?
<--- Score

79. What is the standard for acceptable social technologies performance?
<--- Score

80. What are you attempting to measure/monitor?
<--- Score

81. What do you stand for--and what are you against?
<--- Score

82. How do senior leaders actions reflect a commitment to the organizations social technologies values?
<--- Score

83. Are the social technologies standards challenging?
<--- Score

84. What other areas of the group might benefit from the social technologies team's improvements, knowledge, and learning?
<--- Score

85. Has the social technologies value of standards been quantified?
<--- Score

86. How will the day-to-day responsibilities for monitoring and continual improvement be transferred from the improvement team to the process owner?
<--- Score

87. Who will be in control?
<--- Score

88. How is change control managed?
<--- Score

89. How will the process owner verify improvement in present and future sigma levels, process capabilities?
<--- Score

90. Will the team be available to assist members in planning investigations?
<--- Score

91. Are you measuring, monitoring and predicting social technologies activities to optimize operations and profitability, and enhancing outcomes?
<--- Score

92. Is there a standardized process?

<--- Score

93. Are documented procedures clear and easy to follow for the operators?
<--- Score

94. Do you monitor the effectiveness of your social technologies activities?
<--- Score

95. Are there documented procedures?
<--- Score

96. How likely is the current social technologies plan to come in on schedule or on budget?
<--- Score

97. How do you encourage people to take control and responsibility?
<--- Score

98. Who controls critical resources?
<--- Score

99. What is the recommended frequency of auditing?
<--- Score

Add up total points for this section:
_ _ _ _ _ = Total points for this section

Divided by: _ _ _ _ _ _ (number of statements answered) = _ _ _ _ _ _
Average score for this section

Transfer your score to the social technologies Index at the beginning of

the Self-Assessment.

CRITERION #7: SUSTAIN:

INTENT: Retain the benefits.

In my belief, the answer to this question is clearly defined:

5 Strongly Agree

4 Agree

3 Neutral

2 Disagree

1 Strongly Disagree

1. If no one would ever find out about your accomplishments, how would you lead differently?
<--- Score

2. How can you become the company that would put you out of business?
<--- Score

3. Who do we want your customers to become?
<--- Score

4. What business benefits will social technologies goals deliver if achieved?
<--- Score

5. Are you using a design thinking approach and integrating Innovation, social technologies Experience, and Brand Value?
<--- Score

6. How important is social technologies to the user organizations mission?
<--- Score

7. In the past year, what have you done (or could you have done) to increase the accurate perception of your company/brand as ethical and honest?
<--- Score

8. Did your employees make progress today?
<--- Score

9. Who do you think the world wants your organization to be?
<--- Score

10. What relationships among social technologies trends do you perceive?
<--- Score

11. What stupid rule would you most like to kill?
<--- Score

12. What is the kind of project structure that would be appropriate for your social technologies project, should it be formal and complex, or can it be less formal and relatively simple?

<--- Score

13. What threat is social technologies addressing?
<--- Score

14. How do you listen to customers to obtain actionable information?
<--- Score

15. What are the short and long-term social technologies goals?
<--- Score

16. Is a social technologies breakthrough on the horizon?
<--- Score

17. What knowledge, skills and characteristics mark a good social technologies project manager?
<--- Score

18. How much does social technologies help?
<--- Score

19. How do you set social technologies stretch targets and how do you get people to not only participate in setting these stretch targets but also that they strive to achieve these?
<--- Score

20. How do you transition from the baseline to the target?
<--- Score

21. How do senior leaders deploy your organizations vision and values through your leadership system, to

the workforce, to key suppliers and partners, and to customers and other stakeholders, as appropriate?
<--- Score

22. Why is social technologies important for you now?
<--- Score

23. Have new benefits been realized?
<--- Score

24. How can you incorporate support to ensure safe and effective use of social technologies into the services that you provide?
<--- Score

25. Do you think you know, or do you know you know ?
<--- Score

26. What management system can you use to leverage the social technologies experience, ideas, and concerns of the people closest to the work to be done?
<--- Score

27. What is the range of capabilities?
<--- Score

28. Who will determine interim and final deadlines?
<--- Score

29. How do customers see your organization?
<--- Score

30. What social technologies skills are most

important?
<--- Score

31. What is the purpose of social technologies in relation to the mission?
<--- Score

32. What goals did you miss?
<--- Score

33. Who is responsible for social technologies?
<--- Score

34. Whom among your colleagues do you trust, and for what?
<--- Score

35. Is your basic point _____ or _____?
<--- Score

36. What are the performance and scale of the social technologies tools?
<--- Score

37. Is a social technologies team work effort in place?
<--- Score

38. How will you know that the social technologies project has been successful?
<--- Score

39. What happens when a new employee joins the organization?
<--- Score

40. What potential megatrends could make your

business model obsolete?
<--- Score

41. What new services of functionality will be implemented next with social technologies ?
<--- Score

42. Operational - will it work?
<--- Score

43. What trophy do you want on your mantle?
<--- Score

44. Is the impact that social technologies has shown?
<--- Score

45. How do you ensure that implementations of social technologies products are done in a way that ensures safety?
<--- Score

46. What does your signature ensure?
<--- Score

47. Can you maintain your growth without detracting from the factors that have contributed to your success?
<--- Score

48. Which social technologies goals are the most important?
<--- Score

49. How do you accomplish your long range social technologies goals?
<--- Score

50. What is the big social technologies idea?
<--- Score

51. Is there any reason to believe the opposite of my current belief?
<--- Score

52. What are specific social technologies rules to follow?
<--- Score

53. Who have you, as a company, historically been when you've been at your best?
<--- Score

54. Who will manage the integration of tools?
<--- Score

55. Think of your social technologies project, what are the main functions?
<--- Score

56. What must you excel at?
<--- Score

57. In retrospect, of the projects that you pulled the plug on, what percent do you wish had been allowed to keep going, and what percent do you wish had ended earlier?
<--- Score

58. What did you miss in the interview for the worst hire you ever made?
<--- Score

59. What are the essentials of internal social technologies management?
<--- Score

60. What projects are going on in the organization today, and what resources are those projects using from the resource pools?
<--- Score

61. Has implementation been effective in reaching specified objectives so far?
<--- Score

62. Who will provide the final approval of social technologies deliverables?
<--- Score

63. What are the gaps in your knowledge and experience?
<--- Score

64. What would you recommend your friend do if he/she were facing this dilemma?
<--- Score

65. Are you paying enough attention to the partners your company depends on to succeed?
<--- Score

66. How do you create buy-in?
<--- Score

67. What happens at your organization when people fail?
<--- Score

68. If your company went out of business tomorrow, would anyone who doesn't get a paycheck here care?
<--- Score

69. Do you have the right capabilities and capacities?
<--- Score

70. What have you done to protect your business from competitive encroachment?
<--- Score

71. How is implementation research currently incorporated into each of your goals?
<--- Score

72. What is it like to work for you?
<--- Score

73. Why is it important to have senior management support for a social technologies project?
<--- Score

74. What you are going to do to affect the numbers?
<--- Score

75. How do you govern and fulfill your societal responsibilities?
<--- Score

76. Why not do social technologies?
<--- Score

77. Can the schedule be done in the given time?

<--- Score

78. Who is responsible for errors?
<--- Score

79. Is there any existing social technologies governance structure?
<--- Score

80. Are you satisfied with your current role? If not, what is missing from it?
<--- Score

81. Is there a work around that you can use?
<--- Score

82. How much contingency will be available in the budget?
<--- Score

83. What is a feasible sequencing of reform initiatives over time?
<--- Score

84. What is the overall talent health of your organization as a whole at senior levels, and for each organization reporting to a member of the Senior Leadership Team?
<--- Score

85. If you got fired and a new hire took your place, what would she do different?
<--- Score

86. How do you provide a safe environment -physically and emotionally?

<--- Score

87. Which individuals, teams or departments will be involved in social technologies?
<--- Score

88. What are the challenges?
<--- Score

89. What would have to be true for the option on the table to be the best possible choice?
<--- Score

90. If you weren't already in this business, would you enter it today? And if not, what are you going to do about it?
<--- Score

91. How do you engage the workforce, in addition to satisfying them?
<--- Score

92. How do you track customer value, profitability or financial return, organizational success, and sustainability?
<--- Score

93. How do you go about securing social technologies?
<--- Score

94. What is the overall business strategy?
<--- Score

95. What is effective social technologies?
<--- Score

96. Which models, tools and techniques are necessary?
<--- Score

97. If you had to leave your organization for a year and the only communication you could have with employees/colleagues was a single paragraph, what would you write?
<--- Score

98. What trouble can you get into?
<--- Score

99. What happens if you do not have enough funding?
<--- Score

100. What are the key enablers to make this social technologies move?
<--- Score

101. Do you say no to customers for no reason?
<--- Score

102. What one word do you want to own in the minds of your customers, employees, and partners?
<--- Score

103. How will you insure seamless interoperability of social technologies moving forward?
<--- Score

104. Why do and why don't your customers like your organization?
<--- Score

105. Do you feel that more should be done in the social technologies area?

<--- Score

106. How do you cross-sell and up-sell your social technologies success?

<--- Score

107. Will there be any necessary staff changes (redundancies or new hires)?

<--- Score

108. How do you maintain social technologies's Integrity?

<--- Score

109. Do you know what you are doing? And who do you call if you don't?

<--- Score

110. How does social technologies integrate with other stakeholder initiatives?

<--- Score

111. Do you think social technologies accomplishes the goals you expect it to accomplish?

<--- Score

112. Is social technologies dependent on the successful delivery of a current project?

<--- Score

113. To whom do you add value?

<--- Score

114. Are you making progress, and are you making progress as social technologies leaders?
<--- Score

115. What social technologies modifications can you make work for you?
<--- Score

116. Are assumptions made in social technologies stated explicitly?
<--- Score

117. What is your question? Why?
<--- Score

118. How do you make it meaningful in connecting social technologies with what users do day-to-day?
<--- Score

119. Who, on the executive team or the board, has spoken to a customer recently?
<--- Score

120. How do you lead with social technologies in mind?
<--- Score

121. Do you have enough freaky customers in your portfolio pushing you to the limit day in and day out?
<--- Score

122. What are internal and external social technologies relations?
<--- Score

123. Are your responses positive or negative?
<--- Score

124. Is social technologies realistic, or are you setting yourself up for failure?
<--- Score

125. How will you ensure you get what you expected?
<--- Score

126. Are there any activities that you can take off your to do list?
<--- Score

127. Who will be responsible for deciding whether social technologies goes ahead or not after the initial investigations?
<--- Score

128. How can you negotiate social technologies successfully with a stubborn boss, an irate client, or a deceitful coworker?
<--- Score

129. Why should people listen to you?
<--- Score

130. What counts that you are not counting?
<--- Score

131. What have been your experiences in defining long range social technologies goals?
<--- Score

132. What are the top 3 things at the forefront of your social technologies agendas for the next 3 years?

<--- Score

133. How are you doing compared to your industry?
<--- Score

134. How do you deal with social technologies changes?
<--- Score

135. How long will it take to change?
<--- Score

136. How do you foster innovation?
<--- Score

137. Can you break it down?
<--- Score

138. Who are the key stakeholders?
<--- Score

139. How do you keep the momentum going?
<--- Score

140. Where can you break convention?
<--- Score

141. What are the potential basics of social technologies fraud?
<--- Score

142. What is the estimated value of the project?
<--- Score

143. Are you changing as fast as the world around

you?

<--- Score

144. What are your personal philosophies regarding social technologies and how do they influence your work?

<--- Score

145. How likely is it that a customer would recommend your company to a friend or colleague?

<--- Score

146. Are the assumptions believable and achievable?

<--- Score

147. If there were zero limitations, what would you do differently?

<--- Score

148. Would you rather sell to knowledgeable and informed customers or to uninformed customers?

<--- Score

149. Can you do all this work?

<--- Score

150. If you find that you havent accomplished one of the goals for one of the steps of the social technologies strategy, what will you do to fix it?

<--- Score

151. Who are your customers?

<--- Score

152. What unique value proposition (UVP) do you offer?

<--- Score

153. Do you have past social technologies successes?
<--- Score

154. If you do not follow, then how to lead?
<--- Score

155. Who else should you help?
<--- Score

156. What are current social technologies paradigms?
<--- Score

157. If you were responsible for initiating and implementing major changes in your organization, what steps might you take to ensure acceptance of those changes?
<--- Score

158. What are you trying to prove to yourself, and how might it be hijacking your life and business success?
<--- Score

159. Political -is anyone trying to undermine this project?
<--- Score

160. Do you see more potential in people than they do in themselves?
<--- Score

161. Who are four people whose careers you have enhanced?
<--- Score

162. What do we do when new problems arise?
<--- Score

163. Do you know who is a friend or a foe?
<--- Score

164. How can you become more high-tech but still be high touch?
<--- Score

165. What are the success criteria that will indicate that social technologies objectives have been met and the benefits delivered?
<--- Score

166. How do you determine the key elements that affect social technologies workforce satisfaction, how are these elements determined for different workforce groups and segments?
<--- Score

167. Are the criteria for selecting recommendations stated?
<--- Score

168. Is maximizing social technologies protection the same as minimizing social technologies loss?
<--- Score

169. What are you challenging?
<--- Score

170. Whose voice (department, ethnic group, women, older workers, etc) might you have missed hearing from in your company, and how might you

**amplify this voice to create positive momentum
for your business?**
<--- Score

**171. What is something you believe that nearly no
one agrees with you on?**
<--- Score

172. What could happen if you do not do it?
<--- Score

**173. When information truly is ubiquitous, when
reach and connectivity are completely global,
when computing resources are infinite, and when
a whole new set of impossibilities are not only
possible, but happening, what will that do to your
business?**
<--- Score

174. What is the craziest thing you can do?
<--- Score

**175. Is the social technologies organization
completing tasks effectively and efficiently?**
<--- Score

176. What is the funding source for this project?
<--- Score

177. What are the rules and assumptions your industry
operates under? What if the opposite were true?
<--- Score

178. What is your social technologies strategy?
<--- Score

179. Have benefits been optimized with all key stakeholders?
<--- Score

180. What may be the consequences for the performance of an organization if all stakeholders are not consulted regarding social technologies?
<--- Score

181. Are you / should you be revolutionary or evolutionary?
<--- Score

182. What will be the consequences to the stakeholder (financial, reputation etc) if social technologies does not go ahead or fails to deliver the objectives?
<--- Score

183. What is your formula for success in social technologies ?
<--- Score

184. What is the source of the strategies for social technologies strengthening and reform?
<--- Score

185. What is an unauthorized commitment?
<--- Score

186. How do you keep records, of what?
<--- Score

187. What role does communication play in the success or failure of a social technologies project?
<--- Score

188. At what moment would you think; Will I get fired?
<--- Score

189. What are your most important goals for the strategic social technologies objectives?
<--- Score

190. Who is responsible for ensuring appropriate resources (time, people and money) are allocated to social technologies?
<--- Score

191. How do you stay inspired?
<--- Score

192. Who uses your product in ways you never expected?
<--- Score

193. How do you assess the social technologies pitfalls that are inherent in implementing it?
<--- Score

194. Who is the main stakeholder, with ultimate responsibility for driving social technologies forward?
<--- Score

195. If your customer were your grandmother, would you tell her to buy what you're selling?
<--- Score

196. Who do you want your customers to become?
<--- Score

197. What was the last experiment you ran?

<--- Score

198. How do you know if you are successful?
<--- Score

199. Why will customers want to buy your organizations products/services?
<--- Score

200. Are new benefits received and understood?
<--- Score

201. Are you maintaining a past–present–future perspective throughout the social technologies discussion?
<--- Score

202. Ask yourself: how would you do this work if you only had one staff member to do it?
<--- Score

203. Will it be accepted by users?
<--- Score

204. What should you stop doing?
<--- Score

205. If you had to rebuild your organization without any traditional competitive advantages (i.e., no killer technology, promising research, innovative product/service delivery model, etcetera), how would your people have to approach their work and collaborate together in order to create the necessary conditions for success?
<--- Score

206. How do you manage social technologies Knowledge Management (KM)?
<--- Score

207. What are the business goals social technologies is aiming to achieve?
<--- Score

208. How do you proactively clarify deliverables and social technologies quality expectations?
<--- Score

209. Do you have an implicit bias for capital investments over people investments?
<--- Score

210. What are the long-term social technologies goals?
<--- Score

211. What are the barriers to increased social technologies production?
<--- Score

212. Were lessons learned captured and communicated?
<--- Score

213. Is it economical; do you have the time and money?
<--- Score

Add up total points for this section:
_ _ _ _ _ = Total points for this section

Divided by: _ _ _ _ _ _ (number of

statements answered) = _ _ _ _ _ _
Average score for this section

Transfer your score to the social
technologies Index at the beginning of
the Self-Assessment.

Social Technologies and Managing Projects, Criteria for Project Managers:

1.0 Initiating Process Group: Social Technologies

1. Contingency planning. if a risk event occurs, what will you do?

2. What are the tools and techniques to be used in each phase?

3. The process to Manage Stakeholders is part of which process group?

4. What communication items need improvement?

5. Are you just doing busywork to pass the time?

6. How well defined and documented were the Social Technologies project management processes you chose to use?

7. What is the stake of others in your Social Technologies project?

8. Who is involved in each phase?

9. During which stage of Risk planning are modeling techniques used to determine overall effects of risks on Social Technologies project objectives for high probability, high impact risks?

10. What are the overarching issues of your organization?

11. How can you make your needs known?

12. During which stage of Risk planning are risks prioritized based on probability and impact?

13. What is the NEXT thing to do?

14. Did the Social Technologies project team have the right skills?

15. What areas were overlooked on this Social Technologies project?

16. Who is behind the Social Technologies project?

17. Specific - is the objective clear in terms of what, how, when, and where the situation will be changed?

18. When must it be done?

19. What do you need to do?

1.1 Project Charter: Social Technologies

20. Are you building in-house ?

21. Who is the sponsor?

22. How will you know that a change is an improvement?

23. What barriers do you predict to your success?

24. Who are the stakeholders?

25. Why Outsource?

26. Social Technologies project deliverables: what is the Social Technologies project going to produce?

27. Assumptions: what factors, for planning purposes, are you considering to be true?

28. Social Technologies project background: what is the primary motivation for this Social Technologies project?

29. Why have you chosen the aim you have set forth?

30. Review the general mission What system will be affected by the improvement efforts?

31. Must Have?

32. When is a charter needed?

33. What are you trying to accomplish?

34. Why executive support?

35. Why do you need to manage scope?

36. What are some examples of a business case?

37. Did your Social Technologies project ask for this?

38. Where does all this information come from?

39. Strategic fit: what is the strategic initiative identifier for this Social Technologies project?

1.2 Stakeholder Register: Social Technologies

40. What are the major Social Technologies project milestones requiring communications or providing communications opportunities?

41. What is the power of the stakeholder?

42. What & Why?

43. How will reports be created?

44. Is your organization ready for change?

45. Who is managing stakeholder engagement?

46. Who wants to talk about Security?

47. How should employers make voices heard?

48. How big is the gap?

49. What opportunities exist to provide communications?

50. How much influence do they have on the Social Technologies project?

1.3 Stakeholder Analysis Matrix: Social Technologies

51. Which conditions out of the control of the management are crucial to contribute for the achievement of the development objective?

52. It developments?

53. Niche target markets?

54. What obstacles does your organization face?

55. What advantages do your organizations stakeholders have?

56. Are the interests in line with the program objectives?

57. Political effects?

58. Philosophy and values?

59. Where are mitigation costs factored in?

60. What makes a person a stakeholder?

61. Timescales, deadlines and pressures?

62. Are they likely to influence the success or failure of your Social Technologies project?

63. What could your organization improve?

64. Cashflow, start-up cash-drain?

65. What is the stakeholders mandate, what is mission?

66. Resource providers; who can provide resources to ensure the implementation of the Social Technologies project?

67. How affected by the problem(s)?

68. Market developments?

69. Will the impacts be local, national or international?

70. What should thwe organizations stakeholders avoid?

2.0 Planning Process Group: Social Technologies

71. What is the critical path for this Social Technologies project, and what is the duration of the critical path?

72. To what extent have the target population and participants made the activities own, taking an active role in it?

73. What will you do?

74. How well do the team follow the chosen processes?

75. What business situation is being addressed?

76. How will users learn how to use the deliverables?

77. How should needs be met?

78. How does activity resource estimation affect activity duration estimation?

79. Does the program have follow-up mechanisms (to verify the quality of the products, punctuality of delivery, etc.) to measure progress in the achievement of the envisaged results?

80. Are the follow-up indicators relevant and do they meet the quality needed to measure the outputs and outcomes of the Social Technologies project?

81. What is the difference between the early schedule and late schedule?

82. How will you know you did it?

83. To what extent has a PMO contributed to raising the quality of the design of the Social Technologies project?

84. How well will the chosen processes produce the expected results?

85. What input will you be required to provide the Social Technologies project team?

86. Do the partners have sufficient financial capacity to keep up the benefits produced by the programme?

87. The Social Technologies project charter is created in which Social Technologies project management process group?

88. In what way has the program contributed towards the issue culture and development included on the public agenda?

2.1 Project Management Plan: Social Technologies

89. How can you best help your organization to develop consistent practices in Social Technologies project management planning stages?

90. If the Social Technologies project management plan is a comprehensive document that guides you in Social Technologies project execution and control, then what should it NOT contain?

91. If the Social Technologies project is complex or scope is specialized, do you have appropriate and/or qualified staff available to perform the tasks?

92. How do you organize the costs in the Social Technologies project management plan?

93. How do you manage time?

94. What went right?

95. Why do you manage integration?

96. Are there any windfall benefits that would accrue to the Social Technologies project sponsor or other parties?

97. Are there any scope changes proposed for a previously authorized Social Technologies project?

98. When is a Social Technologies project

management plan created?

99. What is risk management?

100. What data/reports/tools/etc. do your PMs need?

101. Are there any Client staffing expectations?

102. What worked well?

103. Development trends and opportunities. What if the positive direction and vision of your organization causes expected trends to change?

104. Are alternatives safe, functional, constructible, economical, reasonable and sustainable?

105. What is the business need?

106. What are the assumptions?

2.2 Scope Management Plan: Social Technologies

107. What is the estimated cost of creating and implementing?

108. Are you meeting with stake holders and team members?

109. Are actuals compared against estimates to analyze and correct variances?

110. Do all stakeholders know how to access this repository and where to find the Social Technologies project documentation?

111. Are meeting minutes captured and sent out after the meeting?

112. Do you keep stake holders informed?

113. Are Social Technologies project team members committed fulltime?

114. Are stakeholders aware and supportive of the principles and practices of modern software estimation?

115. Are you doing what you have set out to do?

116. How much money have you spent?

117. Has a provision been made to reassess

Social Technologies project risks at various Social Technologies project stages?

118. Is quality monitored from the perspective of the customers needs and expectations?

119. Which statement about customer expectations is not true?

120. Are agendas created for each meeting with meeting objectives, meeting topics, invitee list, and action items from past meetings?

121. The greatest degree of uncertainty is encountered during which phase of the Social Technologies project life cycle?

122. Is there any form of automated support for Issues Management?

123. Pareto diagrams, statistical sampling, flow charting or trend analysis used quality monitoring?

124. What does the critical path really mean?

125. What are the risks that could significantly affect the resources needed for the Social Technologies project?

126. Are measurements and feedback mechanisms incorporated in tracking work effort & refining work estimating techniques?

2.3 Requirements Management Plan: Social Technologies

127. Will the contractors involved take full responsibility?

128. Will the Social Technologies project requirements become approved in writing?

129. Do you understand the role that each stakeholder will play in the requirements process?

130. Did you get proper approvals?

131. The wbs is developed as part of a joint planning session. and how do you know that youhave done this right?

132. To see if a requirement statement is sufficiently well-defined, read it from the developers perspective. Mentally add the phrase, call me when youre done to the end of the requirement and see if that makes you nervous. In other words, would you need additional clarification from the author to understand the requirement well enough to design and implement it?

133. Describe the process for rejecting the Social Technologies project requirements. Who has the authority to reject Social Technologies project requirements?

134. Why manage requirements?

135. Did you distinguish the scope of work the contractor(s) will be required to do?

136. Is it new or replacing an existing business system or process?

137. Should you include sub-activities?

138. Which hardware or software, related to, or as outcome of the Social Technologies project is new to your organization?

139. Did you avoid subjective, flowery or non-specific statements?

140. How will you develop the schedule of requirements activities?

141. Do you know which stakeholders will participate in the requirements effort?

142. What is a problem?

143. What went wrong?

144. Who will perform the analysis?

145. Is requirements work dependent on any other specific Social Technologies project or non-Social Technologies project activities (e.g. funding, approvals, procurement)?

146. Is there formal agreement on who has authority to approve a change in requirements?

2.4 Requirements Documentation: Social Technologies

147. Is your business case still valid?

148. Where are business rules being captured?

149. Do your constraints stand?

150. How can you document system requirements?

151. Does the system provide the functions which best support the customers needs?

152. What are the attributes of a customer?

153. Consistency. are there any requirements conflicts?

154. Can the requirement be changed without a large impact on other requirements?

155. Are there legal issues?

156. Who is interacting with the system?

157. Where do you define what is a customer, what are the attributes of customer?

158. What can tools do for us?

159. Is the requirement properly understood?

160. Basic work/business process; high-level, what is being touched?

161. How much testing do you need to do to prove that your system is safe?

162. What will be the integration problems?

163. How do you get the user to tell you what they want?

164. Are all functions required by the customer included?

165. What is the risk associated with the technology?

166. Completeness. are all functions required by the customer included?

2.5 Requirements Traceability Matrix: Social Technologies

167. Why do you manage scope?

168. Is there a requirements traceability process in place?

169. Why use a WBS?

170. Do you have a clear understanding of all subcontracts in place?

171. How do you manage scope?

172. What is the WBS?

173. Describe the process for approving requirements so they can be added to the traceability matrix and Social Technologies project work can be performed. Will the Social Technologies project requirements become approved in writing?

174. What are the chronologies, contingencies, consequences, criteria?

175. Will you use a Requirements Traceability Matrix?

176. How will it affect the stakeholders personally in career?

177. How small is small enough?

178. What percentage of Social Technologies projects are producing traceability matrices between requirements and other work products?

2.6 Project Scope Statement: Social Technologies

179. Will the risk status be reported to management on a regular and frequent basis?

180. Was planning completed before the Social Technologies project was initiated?

181. Did your Social Technologies project ask for this?

182. Is the plan for Social Technologies project resources adequate?

183. What should you drop in order to add something new?

184. What is change?

185. Will tasks be marked complete only after QA has been successfully completed?

186. What are the defined meeting materials?

187. Write a brief purpose statement for this Social Technologies project. Include a business justification statement. What is the product of this Social Technologies project?

188. Change management vs. change leadership - what is the difference?

189. Elements that deal with providing the detail?

190. Is the quality function identified and assigned?

191. Relevant - ask yourself can you get there; why are you doing this Social Technologies project?

192. If there is an independent oversight contractor, have they signed off on the Social Technologies project Plan?

193. Any new risks introduced or old risks impacted. Are there issues that could affect the existing requirements for the result, service, or product if the scope changes?

194. Once its defined, what is the stability of the Social Technologies project scope?

195. Identify how your team and you will create the Social Technologies project scope statement and the work breakdown structure (WBS). Document how you will create the Social Technologies project scope statement and WBS, and make sure you answer the following questions: In defining Social Technologies project scope and the WBS, will you and your Social Technologies project team be using methods defined by your organization, methods defined by the Social Technologies project management office (PMO), or other methods?

196. Have the configuration management functions been assigned?

2.7 Assumption and Constraint Log: Social Technologies

197. How relevant is this attribute to this Social Technologies project or audit?

198. Are formal code reviews conducted?

199. Does a specific action and/or state that is known to violate security policy occur?

200. Can the requirements be traced to the appropriate components of the solution, as well as test scripts?

201. Are there ways to reduce the time it takes to get something approved?

202. When can log be discarded?

203. Have the scope, objectives, costs, benefits and impacts been communicated to all involved and/or impacted stakeholders and work groups?

204. What threats might prevent you from getting there?

205. How do you design an auditing system?

206. If appropriate, is the deliverable content consistent with current Social Technologies project documents and in compliance with the Document Management Plan?

207. Does the Social Technologies project have a formal Social Technologies project Plan?

208. What would you gain if you spent time working to improve this process?

209. Does a documented Social Technologies project organizational policy & plan (i.e. governance model) exist?

210. Would known impacts serve as impediments?

211. Does the document/deliverable meet general requirements (for example, statement of work) for all deliverables?

212. Have adequate resources been provided by management to ensure Social Technologies project success?

213. Do documented requirements exist for all critical components and areas, including technical, business, interfaces, performance, security and conversion requirements?

214. What to do at recovery?

215. Does the traceability documentation describe the tool and/or mechanism to be used to capture traceability throughout the life cycle?

216. How many Social Technologies project staff does this specific process affect?

2.8 Work Breakdown Structure: Social Technologies

217. Who has to do it?

218. Why would you develop a Work Breakdown Structure?

219. What has to be done?

220. How many levels?

221. How big is a work-package?

222. What is the probability of completing the Social Technologies project in less that xx days?

223. Why is it useful?

224. When do you stop?

225. Where does it take place?

226. Is the work breakdown structure (wbs) defined and is the scope of the Social Technologies project clear with assigned deliverable owners?

227. How much detail?

228. When does it have to be done?

229. Is it a change in scope?

230. When would you develop a Work Breakdown Structure?

231. How far down?

232. How will you and your Social Technologies project team define the Social Technologies projects scope and work breakdown structure?

233. Can you make it?

2.9 WBS Dictionary: Social Technologies

234. Is undistributed budget limited to contract effort which cannot yet be planned to CWBS elements at or below the level specified for reporting to the Government?

235. Are the contractors estimates of costs at completion reconcilable with cost data reported to us?

236. Does the contractor have procedures which permit identification of recurring or non-recurring costs as necessary?

237. Wbs elements contractually specified for reporting of status to you (lowest level only)?

238. Software specification, development, integration, and testing, licenses ?

239. The already stated responsible for overhead performance control of related costs?

240. Does the contractors system include procedures for measuring the performance of critical subcontractors?

241. Are current work performance indicators and goals relatable to original goals as modified by contractual changes, replanning, and reprogramming actions?

242. Are the rates for allocating costs from each indirect cost pool to contracts updated as necessary to ensure a realistic monthly allocation of indirect costs without significant year-end adjustments?

243. Are retroactive changes to budgets for completed work specifically prohibited in an established procedure, and is this procedure adhered to?

244. Does the contractors system provide unit or lot costs when applicable?

245. Are significant decision points, constraints, and interfaces identified as key milestones?

246. Evaluate the performance of operating organizations?

247. Changes in the nature of the overhead requirements?

248. Do the lines of authority for incurring indirect costs correspond to the lines of responsibility for management control of the same components of costs?

249. Are overhead budgets and costs being handled according to the disclosure statement when applicable, or otherwise properly classified (for example, engineering overhead, IR&D)?

250. Incurrence of actual indirect costs in excess of budgets, by element of expense?

251. Are material costs reported within the same period as that in which BCWP is earned for that material?

252. Are estimates of costs at completion utilized in determining contract funding requirements and reporting them?

2.10 Schedule Management Plan: Social Technologies

253. What strengths do you have?

254. Have stakeholder accountabilities & responsibilities been clearly defined?

255. Is pert / critical path or equivalent methodology being used?

256. Are enough systems & user personnel assigned to the Social Technologies project?

257. Does the Social Technologies project have a Quality Culture?

258. Is the communication plan being followed?

259. Are there checklists created to determine if all quality processes are followed?

260. Are changes in scope (deliverable commitments) agreed to by all affected groups & individuals?

261. Has the Social Technologies project manager been identified?

262. Does the schedule have reasonable float?

263. Are the primary and secondary schedule tools defined?

264. Has a structured approach been used to break work effort into manageable components (WBS)?

265. Have external dependencies been captured in the schedule?

266. Are the processes for schedule assessment and analysis defined?

267. Are vendor invoices audited for accuracy before payment?

268. Have reserves been created to address risks?

269. Is the critical path valid?

270. Why time management?

271. Is there an issues management plan in place?

272. Can be realistically shortened (the duration of subsequent tasks)?

2.11 Activity List: Social Technologies

273. What is the probability the Social Technologies project can be completed in xx weeks?

274. How difficult will it be to do specific activities on this Social Technologies project?

275. How will it be performed?

276. What is the total time required to complete the Social Technologies project if no delays occur?

277. What is the LF and LS for each activity?

278. What are you counting on?

279. What are the critical bottleneck activities?

280. Can you determine the activity that must finish, before this activity can start?

281. In what sequence?

282. What went well?

283. When will the work be performed?

284. Where will it be performed?

285. Who will perform the work?

286. How do you determine the late start (LS) for each activity?

287. How much slack is available in the Social Technologies project?

288. What will be performed?

289. When do the individual activities need to start and finish?

290. For other activities, how much delay can be tolerated?

2.12 Activity Attributes: Social Technologies

291. How difficult will it be to do specific activities on this Social Technologies project?

292. How many resources do you need to complete the work scope within a limit of X number of days?

293. Is there a trend during the year?

294. Activity: what is Missing?

295. Activity: what is In the Bag?

296. Do you feel very comfortable with your prediction?

297. Were there other ways you could have organized the data to achieve similar results?

298. Are the required resources available or need to be acquired?

299. How else could the items be grouped?

300. How difficult will it be to complete specific activities on this Social Technologies project?

301. Where else does it apply?

302. Are the required resources available?

303. How many days do you need to complete the work scope with a limit of X number of resources?

304. Has management defined a definite timeframe for the turnaround or Social Technologies project window?

305. Which method produces the more accurate cost assignment?

306. Time for overtime?

307. What is missing?

2.13 Milestone List: Social Technologies

308. Which path is the critical path?

309. Usps (unique selling points)?

310. Effects on core activities, distraction?

311. How late can each activity be finished and started?

312. Continuity, supply chain robustness?

313. Calculate how long can activity be delayed?

314. When will the Social Technologies project be complete?

315. Milestone pages should display the UserID of the person who added the milestone. Does a report or query exist that provides this audit information?

316. Sustainable financial backing?

317. How soon can the activity finish?

318. How will the milestone be verified?

319. Marketing - reach, distribution, awareness?

320. Can you derive how soon can the whole Social Technologies project finish?

321. Loss of key staff?

322. Environmental effects?

323. How late can the activity start?

324. What is your organizations history in doing similar activities?

325. Vital contracts and partners?

2.14 Network Diagram: Social Technologies

326. What to do and When?

327. How difficult will it be to do specific activities on this Social Technologies project?

328. What are the tools?

329. Which type of network diagram allows you to depict four types of dependencies?

330. If x is long, what would be the completion time if you break x into two parallel parts of y weeks and z weeks?

331. What activity must be completed immediately before this activity can start?

332. Will crashing x weeks return more in benefits than it costs?

333. If the Social Technologies project network diagram cannot change and you have extra personnel resources, what is the BEST thing to do?

334. What activities must occur simultaneously with this activity?

335. What job or jobs could run concurrently?

336. Are the gantt chart and/or network diagram

updated periodically and used to assess the overall Social Technologies project timetable?

337. What controls the start and finish of a job?

338. Where do schedules come from?

339. Exercise: what is the probability that the Social Technologies project duration will exceed xx weeks?

340. What must be completed before an activity can be started?

341. What activities must follow this activity?

342. Why must you schedule milestones, such as reviews, throughout the Social Technologies project?

343. Are you on time?

344. What job or jobs precede it?

2.15 Activity Resource Requirements: Social Technologies

345. Which logical relationship does the PDM use most often?

346. What is the Work Plan Standard?

347. Are there unresolved issues that need to be addressed?

348. Is there anything planned that does not need to be here?

349. Other support in specific areas?

350. Organizational Applicability?

351. What are constraints that you might find during the Human Resource Planning process?

352. Anything else?

353. Do you use tools like decomposition and rolling-wave planning to produce the activity list and other outputs?

354. How many signatures do you require on a check and does this match what is in your policy and procedures?

355. How do you handle petty cash?

356. When does monitoring begin?

357. Why do you do that?

2.16 Resource Breakdown Structure: Social Technologies

358. What is the difference between % Complete and % work?

359. When do they need the information?

360. What is Social Technologies project communication management?

361. How difficult will it be to do specific activities on this Social Technologies project?

362. What is each stakeholders desired outcome for the Social Technologies project?

363. Which resources should be in the resource pool?

364. Who will use the system?

365. Goals for the Social Technologies project. What is each stakeholders desired outcome for the Social Technologies project?

366. Changes based on input from stakeholders?

367. What defines a successful Social Technologies project?

368. Who delivers the information?

369. What is the number one predictor of a groups

productivity?

370. What are the requirements for resource data?

371. What is the primary purpose of the human resource plan?

372. Which resource planning tool provides information on resource responsibility and accountability?

373. Who is allowed to see what data about which resources?

374. Who will be used as a Social Technologies project team member?

375. The list could probably go on, but, the thing that you would most like to know is, How long & How much?

2.17 Activity Duration Estimates: Social Technologies

376. Social Technologies project manager is using weighted average duration estimates to perform schedule network analysis. Which type of mathematical analysis is being used?

377. What are the three main outputs of quality control?

378. How much time is required to develop it?

379. What is the duration of a milestone?

380. Are team building activities completed to improve team performance?

381. Who will provide training for the new application?

382. Do stakeholders follow a procedure for formally accepting the Social Technologies project scope?

383. Are changes to the scope managed according to defined procedures?

384. Who will provide inputs for it?

385. Are Social Technologies project activities decomposed into manageable components to ensure expected management control?

386. What is the shortest possible time it will take to complete this Social Technologies project?

387. After how many days will the lease cost be the same as the purchase cost for the equipment?

388. How many different communications channels does a Social Technologies project team with six people have?

389. Is earned value analysis completed to assess Social Technologies project performance?

390. Are activity dependencies documented?

391. Which suggestions do you find most useful?

392. What tasks can take place concurrently?

2.18 Duration Estimating Worksheet: Social Technologies

393. What is next?

394. When does your organization expect to be able to complete it?

395. Small or large Social Technologies project?

396. What is an Average Social Technologies project?

397. Define the work as completely as possible. What work will be included in the Social Technologies project?

398. What is cost and Social Technologies project cost management?

399. What is the total time required to complete the Social Technologies project if no delays occur?

400. Is this operation cost effective?

401. Science = process: remember the scientific method?

402. How should ongoing costs be monitored to try to keep the Social Technologies project within budget?

403. Is the Social Technologies project responsive to community need?

404. What work will be included in the Social Technologies project?

405. What utility impacts are there?

406. What questions do you have?

407. Why estimate time and cost?

408. What is your role?

2.19 Project Schedule: Social Technologies

409. Why do you need schedules?

410. Month Social Technologies project take?

411. How can you minimize or control changes to Social Technologies project schedules?

412. Why do you think schedule issues often cause the most conflicts on Social Technologies projects?

413. Does the condition or event threaten the Social Technologies projects objectives in any ways?

414. Did the Social Technologies project come in under budget?

415. How effectively were issues able to be resolved without impacting the Social Technologies project Schedule or Budget?

416. How closely did the initial Social Technologies project Schedule compare with the actual schedule?

417. How much slack is available in the Social Technologies project?

418. Are procedures defined by which the Social Technologies project schedule may be changed?

419. Verify that the update is accurate. Are all

remaining durations correct?

420. Did the final product meet or exceed user expectations?

421. What is the most mis-scheduled part of process?

422. Master Social Technologies project schedule?

423. Have all Social Technologies project delays been adequately accounted for, communicated to all stakeholders and adjustments made in overall Social Technologies project schedule?

424. Why do you need to manage Social Technologies project Risk?

425. How does a Social Technologies project get to be a year late ?

426. Eliminate unnecessary activities. Are there activities that came from a template or previous Social Technologies project that are not applicable on this phase of this Social Technologies project?

427. Are there activities that came from a template or previous Social Technologies project that are not applicable on this phase of this Social Technologies project?

428. How can you shorten the schedule?

2.20 Cost Management Plan: Social Technologies

429. Is there a formal set of procedures supporting Issues Management?

430. What would you do differently what did not work?

431. Similar Social Technologies projects?

432. Does the schedule include Social Technologies project management time and change request analysis time?

433. Is there an approved case?

434. Risk Analysis?

435. Published materials?

436. Scope of work – What is the likelihood and extent of potential future changes to the Social Technologies project scope?

437. Is it possible to track all classes of Social Technologies project work (e.g. scheduled, un-scheduled, defect repair, etc.)?

438. Contingency rundown curve be used on the Social Technologies project?

439. Sensitivity analysis?

440. Does all Social Technologies project documentation reside in a common repository for easy access?

441. What is an Acceptance Management Process?

442. Are adequate resources provided for the quality assurance function?

443. Was the Social Technologies project schedule reviewed by all stakeholders and formally accepted?

444. Are parking lot items captured?

2.21 Activity Cost Estimates: Social Technologies

445. What areas were overlooked on this Social Technologies project?

446. How do you allocate indirect costs to activities?

447. Will you need to provide essential services information about activities?

448. Based on your Social Technologies project communication management plan, what worked well?

449. Was it performed on time?

450. Was the consultant knowledgeable about the program?

451. If you are asked to lower your estimate because the price is too high, what are your options?

452. How do you change activities?

453. How many activities should you have?

454. How and when do you enter into Social Technologies project Procurement Management?

455. Did the consultant work with local staff to develop local capacity?

456. What is procurement?

457. What areas does the group agree are the biggest success on the Social Technologies project?

458. What cost data should be used to estimate costs during the 2-year follow-up period?

459. Were the tasks or work products prepared by the consultant useful?

460. What is the activity inventory?

461. Can you delete activities or make them inactive?

2.22 Cost Estimating Worksheet: Social Technologies

462. Who is best positioned to know and assist in identifying corresponding factors?

463. Can a trend be established from historical performance data on the selected measure and are the criteria for using trend analysis or forecasting methods met?

464. Identify the timeframe necessary to monitor progress and collect data to determine how the selected measure has changed?

465. What costs are to be estimated?

466. Is the Social Technologies project responsive to community need?

467. What info is needed?

468. How will the results be shared and to whom?

469. Will the Social Technologies project collaborate with the local community and leverage resources?

470. Value pocket identification & quantification what are value pockets?

471. What is the estimated labor cost today based upon this information?

472. What will others want?

473. What can be included?

474. What additional Social Technologies project(s) could be initiated as a result of this Social Technologies project?

475. Is it feasible to establish a control group arrangement?

476. What happens to any remaining funds not used?

477. Does the Social Technologies project provide innovative ways for stakeholders to overcome obstacles or deliver better outcomes?

478. Ask: are others positioned to know, are others credible, and will others cooperate?

479. What is the purpose of estimating?

2.23 Cost Baseline: Social Technologies

480. What is cost and Social Technologies project cost management?

481. Have all approved changes to the Social Technologies project requirement been identified and impact on the performance, cost, and schedule baselines documented?

482. Is there anything you need from upper management in order to be successful?

483. How concrete were original objectives?

484. Have all approved changes to the schedule baseline been identified and impact on the Social Technologies project documented?

485. What weaknesses do you have?

486. Have you identified skills that are missing from your team?

487. Should a more thorough impact analysis be conducted?

488. How accurate do cost estimates need to be?

489. Is there anything unique in this Social Technologies projects scope statement that will affect resources?

490. Has operations management formally accepted responsibility for operating and maintaining the product(s) or service(s) delivered by the Social Technologies project?

491. Is the requested change request a result of changes in other Social Technologies project(s)?

492. If you sold 10x widgets on a day, what would the affect on profits be?

493. What can go wrong?

494. What would the life cycle costs be?

495. Review your risk triggers -have your risks changed?

496. Vac -variance at completion, how much over/ under budget do you expect to be?

497. Has the documentation relating to operation and maintenance of the product(s) or service(s) been delivered to, and accepted by, operations management?

498. Have the actual milestone completion dates been compared to the approved schedule?

2.24 Quality Management Plan: Social Technologies

499. What other teams / processes would be impacted by changes to the current process, and how?

500. How does your organization recruit, hire, and retain new employees?

501. What is the Difference Between a QMP and QAPP?

502. What data do you gather/use/compile?

503. How is the information recorded?

504. Who else should be involved ?

505. Does the Social Technologies project have a formal Social Technologies project Plan?

506. Does the program use modeling in the permitting or decision-making processes?

507. What is the return on investment?

508. Methodology followed?

509. List your organizations customer contact standards that employees are expected to maintain. How are corresponding standards measured?

510. Are there nonconformance issues?

511. How do senior leaders create an environment that encourages learning and innovation?

512. How do you ensure that your sampling methods and procedures meet your data quality objectives?

513. How do you measure?

514. Can it be done better?

515. What has the QM Collaboration done?

516. How does your organization measure customer satisfaction/dissatisfaction?

517. How do you manage quality?

518. How do you ensure that protocols are up to date?

2.25 Quality Metrics: Social Technologies

519. Is quality culture a competitive advantage?

520. Do the operators focus on determining; is there anything you need to worry about?

521. What can manufacturing professionals do to ensure quality is seen as an integral part of the entire product lifecycle?

522. Was review conducted per standard protocols?

523. How should customers provide input?

524. Were number of defects identified?

525. What metrics are important and most beneficial to measure?

526. How do you know if everyone is trying to improve the right things?

527. How do you calculate corresponding metrics?

528. What method of measurement do you use?

529. Does risk analysis documentation meet standards?

530. Are interface issues coordinated?

531. What is the benchmark?

532. Were quality attributes reported?

533. Is there a set of procedures to capture, analyze and act on quality metrics?

534. Where did complaints, returns and warranty claims come from?

535. Should a modifier be included?

536. Do you know how much profit a 10% decrease in waste would generate?

537. How are requirements conflicts resolved?

2.26 Process Improvement Plan: Social Technologies

538. Have storage and access mechanisms and procedures been determined?

539. Are you meeting the quality standards?

540. If a process improvement framework is being used, which elements will help the problems and goals listed?

541. Are there forms and procedures to collect and record the data?

542. Has the time line required to move measurement results from the points of collection to databases or users been established?

543. Where do you want to be?

544. Why do you want to achieve the goal?

545. Does explicit definition of the measures exist?

546. Are you following the quality standards?

547. Management commitment at all levels?

548. What personnel are the coaches for your initiative?

549. Are you making progress on the improvement

framework?

550. Purpose of goal: the motive is determined by asking, why do you want to achieve this goal?

551. Who should prepare the process improvement action plan?

552. Are you making progress on the goals?

553. Where are you now?

554. Everyone agrees on what process improvement is, right?

2.27 Responsibility Assignment Matrix: Social Technologies

555. Are indirect costs accumulated for comparison with the corresponding budgets?

556. Are others working on the right things?

557. Time-phased control account budgets?

558. Identify and isolate causes of favorable and unfavorable cost and schedule variances?

559. Do managers and team members provide helpful suggestions during review meetings?

560. Who is responsible for work and budgets for each wbs?

561. What can you do to improve productivity?

562. Major functional areas of contract effort?

563. What do you do when people do not respond?

564. Availability – will the group or the person be available within the necessary time interval?

565. How many hours by each staff member/rate?

566. Are overhead cost budgets established for each organization which has authority to incur overhead costs?

567. Will too many Communicating responsibilities tangle the Social Technologies project in unnecessary communications?

568. Direct labor dollars and/or hours?

569. What are the assigned resources?

570. Identify potential or actual budget-based and time-based schedule variances?

571. Are work packages assigned to performing organizations?

2.28 Roles and Responsibilities: Social Technologies

572. What specific behaviors did you observe?

573. Concern: where are you limited or have no authority, where you can not influence?

574. Who is involved?

575. Who is responsible for implementation activities and where will the functions, roles and responsibilities be defined?

576. What expectations were met?

577. Key conclusions and recommendations: Are conclusions and recommendations relevant and acceptable?

578. Do you take the time to clearly define roles and responsibilities on Social Technologies project tasks?

579. Who is responsible for each task?

580. Was the expectation clearly communicated?

581. What areas of supervision are challenging for you?

582. Does the team have access to and ability to use data analysis tools?

583. Once the responsibilities are defined for the Social Technologies project, have the deliverables, roles and responsibilities been clearly communicated to every participant?

584. How is your work-life balance?

585. What should you do now to ensure that you are exceeding expectations and excelling in your current position?

586. Do the values and practices inherent in the culture of your organization foster or hinder the process?

587. Are governance roles and responsibilities documented?

588. What expectations were NOT met?

589. Authority: what areas/Social Technologies projects in your work do you have the authority to decide upon and act on the already stated decisions?

590. Is there a training program in place for stakeholders covering expectations, roles and responsibilities and any addition knowledge others need to be good stakeholders?

591. What are your major roles and responsibilities in the area of performance measurement and assessment?

2.29 Human Resource Management Plan: Social Technologies

592. Is the current culture aligned with the vision, mission, and values of the department?

593. Are status reports received per the Social Technologies project Plan?

594. What were things that you did well, and could improve, and how?

595. Are the right people being attracted and retained to meet the future challenges?

596. Have process improvement efforts been completed before requirements efforts begin?

597. Are the appropriate IT resources adequate to meet planned commitments?

598. Were Social Technologies project team members involved in detailed estimating and scheduling?

599. Has a provision been made to reassess Social Technologies project risks at various Social Technologies project stages?

600. Are estimating assumptions and constraints captured?

601. Has a Social Technologies project Communications Plan been developed?

602. Have all involved Social Technologies project stakeholders and work groups committed to the Social Technologies project?

603. How complete is the human resource management plan?

604. Do you have the reasons why the changes to your organizational systems and capabilities are required?

605. Based on your Social Technologies project communication management plan, what worked well?

606. How are you going to ensure that you have a well motivated workforce?

607. Are non-critical path items updated and agreed upon with the teams?

608. Are internal Social Technologies project status meetings held at reasonable intervals?

609. How to convince employees that this is a necessary process?

610. Have all unresolved risks been documented?

2.30 Communications Management Plan: Social Technologies

611. Who is the stakeholder?

612. Is there an important stakeholder who is actively opposed and will not receive messages?

613. What help do you and your team need from the stakeholder?

614. Are there potential barriers between the team and the stakeholder?

615. Will messages be directly related to the release strategy or phases of the Social Technologies project?

616. How were corresponding initiatives successful?

617. How do you manage communications?

618. How will the person responsible for executing the communication item be notified?

619. Do you prepare stakeholder engagement plans?

620. Do you ask; can you recommend others for you to talk with about this initiative?

621. Where do team members get information?

622. Who is involved as you identify stakeholders?

623. Why is stakeholder engagement important?

624. Are there common objectives between the team and the stakeholder?

625. Which team member will work with each stakeholder?

626. In your work, how much time is spent on stakeholder identification?

627. Do you feel more overwhelmed by stakeholders?

628. Who did you turn to if you had questions?

2.31 Risk Management Plan: Social Technologies

629. Market risk -will the new service or product be useful to your organization or marketable to others?

630. Are the metrics meaningful and useful?

631. Are you working on the right risks?

632. For software; does the software interface with new or unproven hardware or unproven vendor products?

633. What are some questions that should be addressed in a risk management plan?

634. Are the reports useful and easy to read?

635. How is the audit profession changing?

636. Which risks should get the attention?

637. Does the software engineering team have the right mix of skills?

638. Are the participants able to keep up with the workload?

639. Is Social Technologies project scope stable?

640. Who has experience with this?

641. Is this an issue, action item, question or a risk?

642. What does a risk management program do?

643. What other risks are created by choosing an avoidance strategy?

644. Does the customer have a solid idea of what is required?

645. What is the likelihood?

646. Could others have been better mitigated?

647. Number of users of the product?

2.32 Risk Register: Social Technologies

648. Who is accountable?

649. What evidence do you have to justify the likelihood score of the risk (audit, incident report, claim, complaints, inspection, internal review)?

650. Recovery actions - planned actions taken once a risk has occurred to allow you to move on. What should you do after?

651. How well are risks controlled?

652. Assume the event happens, what is the Most Likely impact?

653. What can be done about it?

654. When is it going to be done?

655. Who needs to know about this?

656. What is your current and future risk profile?

657. When will it happen?

658. User involvement: do you have the right users?

659. What are the assumptions and current status that support the assessment of the risk?

660. Assume the risk event or situation happens, what would the impact be?

661. How are risks identified?

662. Having taken action, how did the responses effect change, and where is the Social Technologies project now?

663. What are you going to do to limit the Social Technologies projects risk exposure due to the identified risks?

664. Budget and schedule: what are the estimated costs and schedules for performing risk-related activities?

665. People risk -are people with appropriate skills available to help complete the Social Technologies project?

666. Risk probability and impact: how will the probabilities and impacts of risk items be assessed?

2.33 Probability and Impact Assessment: Social Technologies

667. Do you have a mechanism for managing change?

668. Does the Social Technologies project team have experience with the technology to be implemented?

669. Are the risk data timely and relevant?

670. Is security a central objective?

671. What is the risk appetite?

672. Who will be responsible for a slippage?

673. Who should be notified of the occurrence of each of the risk indicators?

674. What will be cost of redeployment of personnel?

675. What are the likely future requirements?

676. Do you use any methods to analyze risks?

677. What are its business ethics?

678. Are team members trained in the use of the tools?

679. What is the impact if the risk does occur?

680. What should be done with non-critical risks?

681. What action do you usually take against risks?

682. What are your data sources?

683. What are the current requirements of the customer?

684. Can this technology be absorbed with current level of expertise available in your organization?

685. Does the software interface with new or unproven hardware or unproven vendor products?

686. Risk may be made during which step of risk management?

2.34 Probability and Impact Matrix: Social Technologies

687. How likely is the current plan to come in on schedule or on budget?

688. What are the methods to deal with risks?

689. How do risks change during the Social Technologies projects life cycle?

690. What can you do about it?

691. How can you understand and diagnose risks and identify sources?

692. How risk averse are you?

693. What should be done with risks on the watch list?

694. Which is the BEST thing to do?

695. Do you have specific methods that you use for each phase of the process?

696. Is Social Technologies project scope stable?

697. Costs associated with late delivery or a defective product?

698. Who is going to be the consortium leader?

699. Have you worked with the customer in the past?

700. Several experts are offsite, and wish to be included. How can this be done?

701. Are formal technical reviews part of this process?

702. Prioritized components/features?

2.35 Risk Data Sheet: Social Technologies

703. What is the chance that it will happen?

704. Do effective diagnostic tests exist?

705. What are your core values?

706. How can hazards be reduced?

707. What is the environment within which you operate (social trends, economic, community values, broad based participation, national directions etc.)?

708. How reliable is the data source?

709. Potential for recurrence?

710. What was measured?

711. Whom do you serve (customers)?

712. What do you know?

713. If it happens, what are the consequences?

714. What are you weak at and therefore need to do better?

715. What do people affected think about the need for, and practicality of preventive measures?

716. What can happen?

717. What will be the consequences if it happens?

718. How can it happen?

719. What actions can be taken to eliminate or remove risk?

720. Risk of what?

2.36 Procurement Management Plan: Social Technologies

721. Are risk oriented checklists used during risk identification?

722. Are the budget estimates reasonable?

723. Does the business case include how the Social Technologies project aligns with your organizations strategic goals & objectives?

724. Is documentation created for communication with the suppliers and Vendors?

725. Are the schedule estimates reasonable given the Social Technologies project?

726. Are updated Social Technologies project time & resource estimates reasonable based on the current Social Technologies project stage?

727. How will multiple providers be managed?

728. Have Social Technologies project management standards and procedures been identified / established and documented?

729. What are your quality assurance overheads?

730. Are staff skills known and available for each task?

731. Is there a procurement management plan in

place?

732. Does the Social Technologies project have a formal Social Technologies project Charter?

733. Is a stakeholder management plan in place that covers topics?

734. Were Social Technologies project team members involved in the development of activity & task decomposition?

735. Are key risk mitigation strategies added to the Social Technologies project schedule?

736. Are Social Technologies project team members involved in detailed estimating and scheduling?

737. Are change requests logged and managed?

738. Measurable - are the targets measurable?

2.37 Source Selection Criteria: Social Technologies

739. Do you have designated specific forms or worksheets?

740. What instructions should be provided regarding oral presentations?

741. What will you use to capture evaluation and subsequent documentation?

742. What are the most common types of rating systems?

743. How and when do you enter into Social Technologies project Procurement Management?

744. What procedures are followed when a contractor requires access to classified information or a significant quantity of special material/information?

745. How much past performance information should be requested?

746. How can business terms and conditions be improved to yield more effective price competition?

747. What should preproposal conferences accomplish?

748. Why promote competition?

749. Are types/quantities of material, facilities appropriate?

750. Do you prepare an independent cost estimate?

751. How are clarifications and communications appropriately used?

752. How do you facilitate evaluation against published criteria?

753. Comparison of each offers prices to the estimated prices -are there significant differences?

754. Will the technical evaluation factor unnecessarily force the acquisition into a higher-priced market segment?

755. Who is on the Source Selection Advisory Committee?

756. What is the last item a Social Technologies project manager must do to finalize Social Technologies project close-out?

757. What aspects should the contracting officer brief the Social Technologies project on prior to evaluation of proposals?

758. When is it appropriate to issue a DRFP?

2.38 Stakeholder Management Plan: Social Technologies

759. Is the current scope of the Social Technologies project substantially different than that originally defined?

760. Were the budget estimates reasonable?

761. Have all involved Social Technologies project stakeholders and work groups committed to the Social Technologies project?

762. Are you meeting your customers expectations consistently?

763. Has a Social Technologies project Communications Plan been developed?

764. Have all stakeholders been identified?

765. Has the budget been baselined?

766. What are the procedures and processes to be followed for purchases, including approval and authorisation requirements?

767. Was trending evident between reviews?

768. Does a documented Social Technologies project organizational policy & plan (i.e. governance model) exist?

769. Who is responsible for accepting the reports produced by the process?

770. How many Social Technologies project staff does this specific process affect?

771. Have activity relationships and interdependencies within tasks been adequately identified?

772. Are there checklists created to demine if all quality processes are followed?

773. Does the Social Technologies project have a Statement of Work?

774. Are tasks tracked by hours?

775. Are schedule deliverables actually delivered?

776. Are Social Technologies project team members involved in detailed estimating and scheduling?

777. Is the steering committee active in Social Technologies project oversight?

778. Are issues raised, assessed, actioned, and resolved in a timely and efficient manner?

2.39 Change Management Plan: Social Technologies

779. When to start change management?

780. What processes are in place to manage knowledge about the Social Technologies project?

781. Have the systems been configured and tested?

782. What is the most positive interpretation it can receive?

783. What are the training strategies?

784. Where will the funds come from?

785. Will a different work structure focus people on what is important?

786. What would be an estimate of the total cost for the activities required to carry out the change initiative?

787. Would you need to tailor a special message for each segment of the audience?

788. Why is the initiative is being undertaken - What are the business drivers?

789. How many people are required in each of the roles?

790. What prerequisite knowledge do corresponding groups need?

791. What does a resilient organization look like?

792. What are the major changes to processes?

793. How do you know the requirements you documented are the right ones?

794. How prevalent is Resistance to Change?

795. What is the most cynical response it can receive?

796. Have the approved procedures and policies been published?

797. What are the responsibilities assigned to each role?

3.0 Executing Process Group: Social Technologies

798. What is the critical path for this Social Technologies project and how long is it?

799. How will professionals learn what is expected from them what the deliverables are?

800. What Social Technologies projects and services are in the portfolio of your organization?

801. How can your organization use a weighted decision matrix to evaluate proposals as part of source selection?

802. What are the main processes included in Social Technologies project quality management?

803. Do Social Technologies project managers understand your organizational context for Social Technologies projects?

804. Are decisions made in a timely manner?

805. Who will provide training?

806. Why do you need a good WBS to use Social Technologies project management software?

807. What is the difference between using brainstorming and the Delphi technique for risk identification?

808. What are the main parts of the scope statement?

809. When is the appropriate time to bring the scorecard to Board meetings?

810. What are deliverables of your Social Technologies project?

811. How can software assist in procuring goods and services?

812. How does Social Technologies project management relate to other disciplines?

813. What are the main types of goods and services being outsourced?

814. How do you enter durations, link tasks, and view critical path information?

815. What were things that you did very well and want to do the same again on the next Social Technologies project?

3.1 Team Member Status Report: Social Technologies

816. How much risk is involved?

817. Why is it to be done?

818. Is there evidence that staff is taking a more professional approach toward management of your organizations Social Technologies projects?

819. Does the product, good, or service already exist within your organization?

820. Are the attitudes of staff regarding Social Technologies project work improving?

821. How can you make it practical?

822. How will resource planning be done?

823. How does this product, good, or service meet the needs of the Social Technologies project and your organization as a whole?

824. Does every department have to have a Social Technologies project Manager on staff?

825. Are your organizations Social Technologies projects more successful over time?

826. Are the products of your organizations Social Technologies projects meeting customers objectives?

827. When a teams productivity and success depend on collaboration and the efficient flow of information, what generally fails them?

828. The problem with Reward & Recognition Programs is that the truly deserving people all too often get left out. How can you make it practical?

829. Do you have an Enterprise Social Technologies project Management Office (EPMO)?

830. What specific interest groups do you have in place?

831. How it is to be done?

832. What is to be done?

833. Does your organization have the means (staff, money, contract, etc.) to produce or to acquire the product, good, or service?

834. Will the staff do training or is that done by a third party?

3.2 Change Request: Social Technologies

835. Who is responsible for the implementation and monitoring of all measures?

836. Describe how modifications, enhancements, defects and/or deficiencies shall be notified (e.g. Problem Reports, Change Requests etc) and managed. Detail warranty and/or maintenance periods?

837. Why do you want to have a change control system?

838. What is the relationship between requirements attributes and attributes like complexity and size?

839. What are the requirements for urgent changes?

840. Are you implementing itil processes?

841. Who can suggest changes?

842. What kind of information about the change request needs to be captured?

843. Who needs to approve change requests?

844. Should staff call into the helpdesk or go to the website?

845. How many lines of code must be changed to

implement the change?

846. What is a Change Request Form?

847. What is the purpose of change control?

848. Who is included in the change control team?

849. How to get changes (code) out in a timely manner?

850. Are there requirements attributes that are strongly related to the occurrence of defects and failures?

851. For which areas does this operating procedure apply?

852. Will new change requests be acknowledged in a timely manner?

3.3 Change Log: Social Technologies

853. Who initiated the change request?

854. Will the Social Technologies project fail if the change request is not executed?

855. Where do changes come from?

856. Is this a mandatory replacement?

857. Is the requested change request a result of changes in other Social Technologies project(s)?

858. Is the change backward compatible without limitations?

859. Is the change request open, closed or pending?

860. How does this relate to the standards developed for specific business processes?

861. When was the request approved?

862. When was the request submitted?

863. How does this change affect the timeline of the schedule?

864. How does this change affect scope?

865. Does the suggested change request seem to represent a necessary enhancement to the product?

866. Does the suggested change request represent a desired enhancement to the products functionality?

867. Is the submitted change a new change or a modification of a previously approved change?

868. Is the change request within Social Technologies project scope?

869. Do the described changes impact on the integrity or security of the system?

3.4 Decision Log: Social Technologies

870. Who is the decisionmaker?

871. How effective is maintaining the log at facilitating organizational learning?

872. How does the use a Decision Support System influence the strategies/tactics or costs?

873. What was the rationale for the decision?

874. Adversarial environment. is your opponent open to a non-traditional workflow, or will it likely challenge anything you do?

875. What eDiscovery problem or issue did your organization set out to fix or make better?

876. Linked to original objective?

877. Behaviors; what are guidelines that the team has identified that will assist them with getting the most out of team meetings?

878. Who will be given a copy of this document and where will it be kept?

879. How consolidated and comprehensive a story can you tell by capturing currently available incident data in a central location and through a log of key decisions during an incident?

880. How does provision of information, both in terms

of content and presentation, influence acceptance of alternative strategies?

881. Does anything need to be adjusted?

882. What is the average size of your matters in an applicable measurement?

883. Which variables make a critical difference?

884. How do you know when you are achieving it?

885. What alternatives/risks were considered?

886. What makes you different or better than others companies selling the same thing?

887. How does an increasing emphasis on cost containment influence the strategies and tactics used?

888. Meeting purpose; why does this team meet?

889. At what point in time does loss become unacceptable?

3.5 Quality Audit: Social Technologies

890. Do all staff have the necessary authority and resources to deliver what is expected of them?

891. Is refuse and garbage adequately stored and disposed of with sufficient frequency to prevent contamination?

892. Are people allowed to contribute ideas?

893. How does your organization know that its management of its ethical responsibilities is appropriately effective and constructive?

894. How does your organization know that the range and quality of its social and recreational services and facilities are appropriately effective and constructive in meeting the needs of staff?

895. Do prior clients have a positive opinion of your organization?

896. How does your organization know that its teaching activities (and staff learning) are effectively and constructively enhanced by its activities?

897. How does your organization know that its relationships with the community at large are appropriately effective and constructive?

898. Is quality audit a prerequisite for program accreditation or program recognition?

899. Are all records associated with the reconditioning of a device maintained for a minimum of two years after the sale or disposal of the last device within a lot of merchandise?

900. What is the collective experience of the team to be assigned to an audit?

901. Do the acceptance procedures and specifications include the criteria for acceptance/rejection, define the process to be used, and specify the measuring and test equipment that is to be used?

902. Are the intentions consistent with external obligations (such as applicable laws)?

903. How does your organization know that its systems for assisting staff with career planning and employment placements are appropriately effective and constructive?

904. How does your organization know that its system for ensuring that its training activities are appropriately resourced and support is appropriately effective and constructive?

905. Do the suppliers use a formal quality system?

906. How do you know what, specifically, is required of you in your work?

907. How does your organization know that its staff embody the core knowledge, skills and characteristics for which it wishes to be recognized?

908. Is the continuing professional education of key

personnel account fored in detail?

909. It is inappropriate to seek information about the Audit Panels preliminary views including questions like why do you ask that?

3.6 Team Directory: Social Technologies

910. Days from the time the issue is identified?

911. Who are the Team Members?

912. Have you decided when to celebrate the Social Technologies projects completion date?

913. How and in what format should information be presented?

914. Process decisions: are all start-up, turn over and close out requirements of the contract satisfied?

915. Process decisions: do job conditions warrant additional actions to collect job information and document on-site activity?

916. Who will talk to the customer?

917. Timing: when do the effects of communication take place?

918. Does a Social Technologies project team directory list all resources assigned to the Social Technologies project?

919. Do purchase specifications and configurations match requirements?

920. Decisions: what could be done better to improve

the quality of the constructed product?

921. Process decisions: are contractors adequately prosecuting the work?

922. Where will the product be used and/or delivered or built when appropriate?

923. Process decisions: which organizational elements and which individuals will be assigned management functions?

924. Who will be the stakeholders on your next Social Technologies project?

925. Process decisions: do invoice amounts match accepted work in place?

926. Who should receive information (all stakeholders)?

927. How do unidentified risks impact the outcome of the Social Technologies project?

928. Who will write the meeting minutes and distribute?

3.7 Team Operating Agreement: Social Technologies

929. How will your group handle planned absences?

930. Are there more than two functional areas represented by your team?

931. What administrative supports will be put in place to support the team and the teams supervisor?

932. Are leadership responsibilities shared among team members (versus a single leader)?

933. Did you prepare participants for the next meeting?

934. What are the current caseload numbers in the unit?

935. To whom do you deliver your services?

936. What is culture?

937. Are there more than two national cultures represented by your team?

938. What types of accommodations will be formulated and put in place for sustaining the team?

939. How will group handle unplanned absences?

940. Resource allocation: how will individual team

members account for time and expenses, and how will this be allocated in the team budget?

941. Have you established procedures that team members can follow to work effectively together, such as a team operating agreement?

942. Do you vary your voice pace, tone and pitch to engage participants and gain involvement?

943. How will you divide work equitably?

944. Did you draft the meeting agenda?

945. Does your team need access to all documents and information at all times?

946. Are there the right people on your team?

947. Do you determine the meeting length and time of day?

948. Do you listen for voice tone and word choice to understand the meaning behind words?

3.8 Team Performance Assessment: Social Technologies

949. To what degree can the team ensure that all members are individually and jointly accountable for the teams purpose, goals, approach, and work-products?

950. How does Social Technologies project termination impact Social Technologies project team members?

951. To what degree are fresh input and perspectives systematically caught and added (for example, through information and analysis, new members, and senior sponsors)?

952. To what degree is the team cognizant of small wins to be celebrated along the way?

953. Do you promptly inform members about major developments that may affect them?

954. To what degree are the relative importance and priority of the goals clear to all team members?

955. To what degree are the goals realistic?

956. To what degree do team members frequently explore the teams purpose and its implications?

957. What is method variance?

958. To what degree are staff involved as partners in the improvement process?

959. What do you think is the most constructive thing that could be done now to resolve considerations and disputes about method variance?

960. If you have received criticism from reviewers that your work suffered from method variance, what was the circumstance?

961. To what degree are sub-teams possible or necessary?

962. How do you manage human resources?

963. Is there a particular method of data analysis that you would recommend as a means of demonstrating that method variance is not of great concern for a given dataset?

964. To what degree can the team measure progress against specific goals?

965. What makes opportunities more or less obvious?

966. How do you encourage members to learn from each other?

967. To what degree does the teams purpose contain themes that are particularly meaningful and memorable?

968. To what degree do team members understand one anothers roles and skills?

3.9 Team Member Performance Assessment: Social Technologies

969. How is your organizations Strategic Management System tied to performance measurement?

970. What kinds of performance factors / elements do you use?

971. To what degree is there a sense that only the team can succeed?

972. Who they are?

973. How often are assessments to be conducted?

974. What changes do you need to make to align practices with beliefs?

975. How do you use data to inform instruction and improve staff achievement?

976. How is assessment information achieved, stored?

977. Is it critical or vital to the job?

978. What makes them effective?

979. What instructional strategies were developed/ incorporated (e.g., direct instruction, indirect instruction, experiential learning, independent study, interactive instruction)?

980. How do you start collaborating?

981. Does adaptive training work?

982. To what degree do team members feel that the purpose of the team is important, if not exciting?

983. To what extent are systems and applications (e.g., game engine, mobile device platform) utilized?

984. Who is responsible?

985. What innovations (if any) are developed to realize goals?

986. To what degree does the teams approach to its work allow for modification and improvement over time?

987. Does the rater (supervisor) have to wait for the interim or final performance assessment review to tell an employee that the employees performance is unsatisfactory?

3.10 Issue Log: Social Technologies

988. Can you think of other people who might have concerns or interests?

989. In classifying stakeholders, which approach to do so are you using?

990. What approaches do you use?

991. Are you constantly rushing from meeting to meeting?

992. Is the issue log kept in a safe place?

993. Can an impact cause deviation beyond team, stage or Social Technologies project tolerances?

994. Why multiple evaluators?

995. What is a change?

996. Are the stakeholders getting the information they need, are they consulted, are concerns addressed?

997. Is access to the Issue Log controlled?

998. Who were proponents/opponents?

999. Which stakeholders can influence others?

1000. What is the impact on the Business Case?

1001. Who needs to know and how much?

1002. What help do you and your team need from the stakeholders?

4.0 Monitoring and Controlling Process Group: Social Technologies

1003. If action is called for, what form should it take?

1004. When will the Social Technologies project be done?

1005. Were decisions made in a timely manner?

1006. Were sponsors and decision makers available when needed outside regularly scheduled meetings?

1007. User: who wants the information and what are they interested in?

1008. Mitigate. what will you do to minimize the impact should a risk event occur?

1009. Propriety: who needs to be involved in the evaluation to be ethical?

1010. How well did the chosen processes produce the expected results?

1011. Where is the Risk in the Social Technologies project?

1012. Is there sufficient funding available for this?

1013. Who are the Social Technologies project stakeholders?

1014. What kinds of things in particular are you looking for data on?

1015. Overall, how does the program function to serve the clients?

1016. How is agile Social Technologies project management done?

1017. In what way has the program come up with innovative measures for problem-solving?

1018. What are the deliverables?

4.1 Project Performance Report: Social Technologies

1019. To what degree does the teams work approach provide opportunity for members to engage in results-based evaluation?

1020. To what degree can team members vigorously define the teams purpose in considerations with others who are not part of the functioning team?

1021. To what degree do the relationships of the informal organization motivate taskrelevant behavior and facilitate task completion?

1022. To what degree are the skill areas critical to team performance present?

1023. To what degree is there centralized control of information sharing?

1024. To what degree do members articulate the goals beyond the team membership?

1025. To what degree will team members, individually and collectively, commit time to help themselves and others learn and develop skills?

1026. How will procurement be coordinated with other Social Technologies project aspects, such as scheduling and performance reporting?

1027. To what degree are the demands of the task

compatible with and converge with the relationships of the informal organization?

1028. What is the PRS?

1029. To what degree does the funding match the requirement?

1030. To what degree are the teams goals and objectives clear, simple, and measurable?

1031. What is the degree to which rules govern information exchange between groups?

1032. To what degree does the informal organization make use of individual resources and meet individual needs?

1033. To what degree are the structures of the formal organization consistent with the behaviors in the informal organization?

1034. To what degree does the formal organization make use of individual resources and meet individual needs?

4.2 Variance Analysis: Social Technologies

1035. How does the use of a single conversion element (rather than the traditional labor and overhead elements) affect standard costing?

1036. Are overhead cost budgets established for each department which has authority to incur overhead costs?

1037. Other relevant issues of Variance Analysis -selling price or gross margin?

1038. The anticipated business volume?

1039. Are the requirements for all items of overhead established by rational, traceable processes?

1040. Are the overhead pools formally and adequately identified?

1041. Is all contract work included in the CWBS?

1042. Does the accounting system provide a basis for auditing records of direct costs chargeable to the contract?

1043. What are the actual costs to date?

1044. Budget versus actual. how does the monthly budget compare to actual experience?

1045. How are material, labor, and overhead standards set?

1046. Are there changes in the direct base to which overhead costs are allocated?

1047. What is the performance to date and material commitment?

1048. Are all authorized tasks assigned to identified organizational elements?

1049. Are there changes in the overhead pool and/or organization structures?

1050. Are all cwbs elements specified for external reporting?

1051. Did a new competitor enter the market?

1052. What is the budgeted cost for work scheduled?

1053. What is exceptional?

4.3 Earned Value Status: Social Technologies

1054. Earned value can be used in almost any Social Technologies project situation and in almost any Social Technologies project environment. it may be used on large Social Technologies projects, medium sized Social Technologies projects, tiny Social Technologies projects (in cut-down form), complex and simple Social Technologies projects and in any market sector. some people, of course, know all about earned value, they have used it for years - but perhaps not as effectively as they could have?

1055. Verification is a process of ensuring that the developed system satisfies the stakeholders agreements and specifications; Are you building the product right? What do you verify?

1056. Are you hitting your Social Technologies projects targets?

1057. Where is evidence-based earned value in your organization reported?

1058. How does this compare with other Social Technologies projects?

1059. How much is it going to cost by the finish?

1060. If earned value management (EVM) is so good in determining the true status of a Social Technologies project and Social Technologies project its completion, why is it that hardly any one uses it in information systems related Social Technologies projects?

1061. Validation is a process of ensuring that the developed system will actually achieve the stakeholders desired outcomes; Are you building the right product? What do you validate?

1062. Where are your problem areas?

1063. What is the unit of forecast value?

1064. When is it going to finish?

4.4 Risk Audit: Social Technologies

1065. Why do audits fail?

1066. When your organization is entering into a major contract, does it seek legal advice?

1067. Do requirements put excessive performance constraints on the product?

1068. What is the anticipated volatility of the requirements?

1069. How do you manage risk?

1070. Are you willing to seek legal advice when required?

1071. Is a software Social Technologies project management tool available?

1072. Have staff received necessary training?

1073. Are the software tools integrated with each other?

1074. What compliance systems do you have in place to address quality, errors, and outcomes?

1075. Do you have proper induction processes for all new paid staff and volunteers who have a specific role and responsibility?

1076. Are requirements fully understood by the team

and customers?

1077. Are regular safety inspections made of buildings, grounds and equipment?

1078. Are you aware of the industry standards that apply to your operations?

1079. Do you have written and signed agreements/ contracts in place for each paid staff member?

1080. Does your organization have a social media policy and procedure?

1081. Is the auditor able to evaluate contradictory evidence in an unbiased manner?

1082. Do you manage the process through use of metrics?

1083. Do you have an emergency plan?

4.5 Contractor Status Report: Social Technologies

1084. If applicable; describe your standard schedule for new software version releases. Are new software version releases included in the standard maintenance plan?

1085. Are there contractual transfer concerns?

1086. Describe how often regular updates are made to the proposed solution. Are corresponding regular updates included in the standard maintenance plan?

1087. What process manages the contracts?

1088. What was the final actual cost?

1089. What are the minimum and optimal bandwidth requirements for the proposed solution?

1090. How does the proposed individual meet each requirement?

1091. What was the budget or estimated cost for your organizations services?

1092. How long have you been using the services?

1093. How is risk transferred?

1094. What was the overall budget or estimated cost?

1095. Who can list a Social Technologies project as organization experience, your organization or a previous employee of your organization?

1096. What is the average response time for answering a support call?

1097. What was the actual budget or estimated cost for your organizations services?

4.6 Formal Acceptance: Social Technologies

1098. Is formal acceptance of the Social Technologies project product documented and distributed?

1099. Was the client satisfied with the Social Technologies project results?

1100. Do you buy pre-configured systems or build your own configuration?

1101. What lessons were learned about your Social Technologies project management methodology?

1102. Do you buy-in installation services?

1103. Have all comments been addressed?

1104. Was the sponsor/customer satisfied?

1105. What function(s) does it fill or meet?

1106. Does it do what Social Technologies project team said it would?

1107. Do you perform formal acceptance or burn-in tests?

1108. Does it do what client said it would?

1109. How well did the team follow the methodology?

1110. Who would use it?

1111. Was the Social Technologies project goal achieved?

1112. What was done right?

1113. Did the Social Technologies project achieve its MOV?

1114. What is the Acceptance Management Process?

1115. What features, practices, and processes proved to be strengths or weaknesses?

1116. Was the Social Technologies project work done on time, within budget, and according to specification?

1117. Was business value realized?

5.0 Closing Process Group: Social Technologies

1118. What were things that you need to improve?

1119. When will the Social Technologies project be done?

1120. Is this an updated Social Technologies project Proposal Document?

1121. Did the Social Technologies project management methodology work?

1122. Can the lesson learned be replicated?

1123. Does the close educate others to improve performance?

1124. Were escalated issues resolved promptly?

1125. What areas were overlooked on this Social Technologies project?

1126. What areas were overlooked on this Social Technologies project?

1127. How well did you do?

1128. Based on your Social Technologies project communication management plan, what worked well?

1129. What could have been improved?

1130. How well did the team follow the chosen processes?

1131. What is the overall risk of the Social Technologies project to your organization?

1132. Did the Social Technologies project team have the right skills?

5.1 Procurement Audit: Social Technologies

1133. Is the procurement Social Technologies project efficiently managed?

1134. Are all checks stored in a secure area?

1135. Was there reasonable justification for the need of the purchase, namely when made towards the end of the financial year?

1136. Are checks used in numeric sequence?

1137. Was the suitability of candidates accurately assessed?

1138. Is the procurement process well organized?

1139. Are procurement processes well organized and documented?

1140. Which contracts have been awarded for works, supply of products or provision of services?

1141. Has an upper limit of cost been fixed?

1142. Are reports based on sound data available to the already stated responsible for monitoring the performance of contracts?

1143. Does the department have a procurement strategy and is it implemented?

1144. Are approval limits covered in written procedures?

1145. Were exclusion causes duly considered before the actual evaluation of tenders?

1146. Are purchase requisitions used to generate purchase orders?

1147. Are there procedures for trade-in arrangements?

1148. When competitive dialogue was used, did the contracting authority provide sufficient justification for the use of this procedure and was the contract actually particularly complex?

1149. Does the procurement function/unit have the ability to apply public procurement principles and to prepare tender and contract documents?

1150. Did the conditions included in the contract protect the risk of non-performance by the supplier and were there no conflicting provisions?

1151. Does the procurement function/unit have the ability to apply electronic procurement?

1152. Is each copy of the purchase order necessary?

5.2 Contract Close-Out: Social Technologies

1153. How/when used ?

1154. What happens to the recipient of services?

1155. Change in circumstances?

1156. Change in knowledge?

1157. Was the contract type appropriate?

1158. What is capture management?

1159. Have all contracts been completed?

1160. Are the signers the authorized officials?

1161. Have all contract records been included in the Social Technologies project archives?

1162. Parties: Authorized?

1163. Parties: who is involved?

1164. How is the contracting office notified of the automatic contract close-out?

1165. Have all contracts been closed?

1166. Has each contract been audited to verify acceptance and delivery?

1167. Have all acceptance criteria been met prior to final payment to contractors?

1168. Was the contract complete without requiring numerous changes and revisions?

1169. Change in attitude or behavior?

1170. Was the contract sufficiently clear so as not to result in numerous disputes and misunderstandings?

1171. How does it work?

5.3 Project or Phase Close-Out: Social Technologies

1172. Planned completion date?

1173. Is the lesson significant, valid, and applicable?

1174. Complete yes or no?

1175. In addition to assessing whether the Social Technologies project was successful, it is equally critical to analyze why it was or was not fully successful. Are you including this?

1176. What is this stakeholder expecting?

1177. Is there a clear cause and effect between the activity and the lesson learned?

1178. What are the mandatory communication needs for each stakeholder?

1179. Was the user/client satisfied with the end product?

1180. What are the informational communication needs for each stakeholder?

1181. What could be done to improve the process?

1182. If you were the Social Technologies project sponsor, how would you determine which Social Technologies project team(s) and/or individuals deserve recognition?

1183. Planned remaining costs?

1184. What advantages do the an individual interview have over a group meeting, and vice-versa?

1185. Who is responsible for award close-out?

1186. How often did each stakeholder need an update?

1187. What benefits or impacts does the stakeholder group expect to obtain as a result of the Social Technologies project?

1188. What were the actual outcomes?

1189. What information is each stakeholder group interested in?

1190. Is the lesson based on actual Social Technologies project experience rather than on independent research?

5.4 Lessons Learned: Social Technologies

1191. What would you like to see better documented about how to use existing processes on this type of Social Technologies project?

1192. How well do you feel the executives supported this Social Technologies project?

1193. How well is the build process working?

1194. How timely were Progress Reports provided to the Social Technologies project Manager by Team Members?

1195. How well does the product or service the Social Technologies project produced meet your needs?

1196. What was the methodology behind successful learning experiences, and how might they be applied to the broader challenge of your organizations knowledge management?

1197. What are the needs of the individuals?

1198. What is the impact of tax policy on the case?

1199. What are the conceptual limits of the research?

1200. How many interest groups are stakeholders?

1201. Were the aims and objectives achieved?

1202. How was the political and social history changed over the life of the Social Technologies project?

1203. How efficient is the deliverable?

1204. What surprises did the team have to deal with?

1205. What were the key issues?

1206. What were the lessons learned on this Social Technologies project?

1207. What would you approach differently next time?

1208. What skills did you need that were missing on this Social Technologies project?

1209. How often do communications get lost?

1210. What is the economic growth rate?

Index

CPSIA information can be obtained
at www.ICGtesting.com
Printed in the USA
BVHW041010200819
556236BV00011B/708/P